THE BATTLE OVER MULTICULTURALISM

Does it help or hinder Canadian unity?

Andrew Cardozo & Louis Musto
(editors)

Volume I

First edition

Canadian Cataloguing in Publication Data
The Battle over Multiculturalism: Does it help or hinder Canadian Identity?

ISBN 0-968 1458-0-9

1. Multiculturalism - Canada. I. Cardozo, Andrew, 1956- II. Musto, Louis, 1961

FC105.M8B381997 305.8'00971 C96-900919.4
F1035.A1B36 1997

We gratefully acknowledge the support of the writers who gave freely of their time, INTERWORKS (Information Technology Specialists), Photocopy Plus, Ltd. Ottawa, and the Department of Canadian Heritage (Multiculturalism Program).

The opinions expressed are those of the authors and do not necessarily reflect the opinions of the Pearson-Shoyama Institute.

For more information:
PSI Publishing
Pearson-Shoyama Institute
219 Argyle Avenue
Ottawa, Ontario K2P 2H4
Phone: (613) 230-8284
Fax: (613) 235-3160

The Pearson-Shoyama Institute is a national non-governmental, non-profit organization that addresses issues of inclusiveness in Canadian society. It promotes dialogue among Canadians around basic Canadian values, undertakes research on various public policies, conducts consultations, and provides training especially around diversity management. The Institute is not an advocacy organization. Its members are free to promote their own personal viewpoints.

Printed in Canada on recycled paper.

For **Leonard J. Cardozo** (1925-1996)
and **Michele Musto** (1923-1995)
who were immigrants
and
proud Canadian citizens.

TABLE OF CONTENTS

Foreward i

Opening Remarks to the Juliet Cuenco Annual Memorial Seminar 1
Amelita A. Armit

DEFINING THE BATTLE LINES

Introduction: Identifying the Issues 7
Andrew Cardozo and Louis Musto

All Over the Map: The Lack of Consensus on Canadian Unity 16
Andrew Cardozo

Public Opinion on Multiculturalism and Canadian Identity 26
Louis Musto

PARLIAMENTARY VIEWS ON NATION BUILDING

Liberal Party: A Continued Commitment to the Ideals of Multiculturalism 35
Hedy Fry

Bloc Québécois: Integration Rather Than Multiculturalism 42
Christiane Gagnon

Reform Party: Federal Funding for Multiculturalism a Needless Expense 46
Cliff Breitkreuz

New Democratic Party: Standing Up for Canadian Values 49
Simon de Jong

Progressive Conservative Party: Guiding Our Future Through an Understanding of the Past 54
Noël A. Kinsella
Independent MP: Culture as an Individual Responsibility 60
Jan Brown

RACE, EQUALITY AND JUSTICE IN CANADA

Multiculturalism, Jews and the Forging of the Canadian Identity 71
Irving Abella
The Role of Ethnic Minorities in the Pursuit of Equality and Multiculturalism 90
Emilio S. Binavince
Our Constitution Does Not Admit of Distinctions of Races 101
Nathan M. Greenfield
True North Strong and Hyphen-Free 111
R.L. Gabrielle Nishiguchi
New Racism, Cultural Diversity and the Search for a National Identity 115
Li Zong

CANADA AND THE WORLD

The Role of Ethnic Minorities in Building a Stronger Economy and a More United Country 129
Jonathan L. Calof
Multiculturalism in Australia, the United States and the United Kingdom: An Overview 137
Karim H. Karim
The Quest for Canadian Unity in a Changing World 143
Geoffrey Pearson

MULTICULTURALISM AS A BUILDING BLOCK

Linking Our Multicultural Asset to the Information Highway 151
Jean Augustine
Defending a Meager Program 158
Amy Go
Quebec, Canada and Multiculturalism: A Vision for the 21st Century 164
Fo Niemi
How to Advance National Unity: A Professional and Personal Perspective 173
C. Lloyd Stanford
Multiculturalism as a Response to an Evolving Society 183
Elliot Tepper
A Must for B.C., A Must for Canada 201
Lilian To
The Only Way to Go: Why Multiculturalism Can Help Unity 207
Joseph Wong

Contributors 213

FOREWARD

The idea for this book originated with the first annual memorial Juliet Cuenco seminar, organized by the Pearson-Shoyama Institute and held on May 27, 1996 in Ottawa.

The topic of discussion, multiculturalism and national unity, generated considerable interest. The federal multiculturalism policy has been in existence for 25 years, yet it continues to face a barrage of attacks. In recent years, multiculturalism has been increasingly linked to the national unity debate. During the seminar, many argued that multiculturalism was about respect for differences, tolerance, integration, the promotion of shared values, and an important symbol of the Canadian identity. Others saw it as divisive, a hindrance to nation building, and a needless area of government involvement.

The original intent was to limit the seminar follow-up to the preparation and distribution of the proceedings to the participants. The topic, however, was far too important to confine the discussion to those who were involved in the seminar. To help engage a broader public discussion, the Pearson-Shoyama Institute, invited 24 Canadians from different walks of life to prepare essays on their views of multiculturalism and national unity. These essays are contained in this first volume.

We are indebted to the contributors to this book. Special thanks are due to Mary O'Neill for her sound editorial advice; to Stephanie David for her patience and help in designing the layout and making the changes to the text; and to Jonathan Calof for assisting with the cover design.

THE PEARSON-SHOYAMA INSTITUTE

OPENING REMARKS TO THE JULIET CUENCO ANNUAL MEMORIAL SEMINAR

Amelita A. Armit

On May 27, 1996, the Pearson-Shoyama Institute held the first Annual Memorial Juliet Cuenco Seminar which addresses issues of diversity in Canada. The title was "Multiculturalism and National Unity: A Vision for the 21st Century." Amelita Armit, a senior public servant and a personal friend of Juliet Cuenco, was the moderator. Her opening remarks most appropriately captured the life of Ms. Cuenco and the reality and vibrancy of the debate around multiculturalism.

It is my great pleasure to moderate the first Juliet Cuenco Annual Memorial Seminar. We have a special gathering tonight and I would like to highlight three features that make it such a fitting tribute to Juliet Cuenco.

First is that it is named in honour of Juliet Cuenco, who lived a life dedicated to the advancement of every individual she touched and every community she belonged to, in her personal, voluntary and professional capacities. Juliet was my contemporary from student days at the University of the Philippines, almost three decades ago. She was the President of her sorority and she was active in university politics and student representation. Even then, she showed an activism permeated with an acute understanding of the human condition and the need to build a community premised on ensuring the dignity of each individual. The threads of our lives got connected again when I moved here to Ottawa in 1987, and by then Juliet had added to the fullness of her life in her devotion to her family. She was very proud of her "three men"—Art, Cazzle and Patrick—and they became partners and co-conspirators in her never ending quest for excellence in one's self and for excellence in service to others.

Juliet was truly a special person: she not only cared about issues and people, she made things happen. And happen they did—in her work as a Program Officer with Canadian Heritage; in her work advancing the cause of immigrant women, in particular the treatment of domestics; in her efforts to mobilize a unified voice for the Filipino community as the first Executive Director of the United Council of Filipino Associations in Canada; and in her insights in launching the Science and Technology Advisory Council to encourage professional Filipino expatriates to lend their expertise back to the Philippines and to establish scholarships to support the development of high-potential Filipinos in science and technology.

The second important feature of this memorial is the theme for the seminar—*Multiculturalism and National Unity: A Vision for the 21st Century* —a theme close to Juliet's heart. To Juliet, multiculturalism and unity were not abstract concepts. Multiculturalism was not a program or initiative; it was a way of life, incorporating values, commitments and processes that went beyond the interests of particular groups and individuals. And she reflected this belief in the programs and strategies she helped develop at Canadian Heritage to give meaning and life to the Multiculturalism Act. Juliet also saw multiculturalism as an instrument for forging a unique Canadian identity. She saw Canada serving as a model of the new world—an interactive, interconnected world, strengthened by the richness of its diverse people resources. That is why she was active not only with the Filipino community but with multicultural communities, the Canadian community as a whole.

But Juliet also knew that multiculturalism was an issue fraught with controversy, myths and misperceptions. Which brings me to the third significant feature of this memorial—the seminar format with a panel of distinguished speakers who will examine the theme from various perspectives. This format is a celebration of Juliet's belief in the power of ideas, dialogue and exchange. She was a consummate practitioner of bringing people together to discuss, debate, listen, and to just have fun being with each other. It was her way of making people understand their similarities and differences, and at the same time recognize their legitimate voices.

For all these reasons, I am delighted that we have all come together to honour Juliet through this annual seminar. Juliet's life and work lives through each of us and we are all the better for it. So let tonight be also a celebration of this legacy.

DEFINING THE BATTLE LINES

INTRODUCTION: IDENTIFYING THE ISSUES

by Andrew Cardozo and Louis Musto

Cultural diversity existed in Canada well before the arrival of European settlers. The Aboriginal and Inuit peoples were here first, and each were composed of sub-groups with their own language, culture and social organization. When the French and English arrived they brought with them their respective culture, language and religion, which they imposed on the people who were here before them, and then on those who came later to our shores from other countries.

People of non-French and non-English origin also brought to Canada their cultures, languages and religions, but did not impose their way of life on those who were here before them. The federal Multiculturalism Policy of 1971 was expected to signal recognition and acceptance of the history of our ethnic and cultural diversity, and to advance and manage all the issues related to this diversity.

Today, the federal Multiculturalism Policy has become the target for an array of discontent and criticisms. When the Pearson-Shoyama Institute organized the first annual Juliet Cuenco Memorial Seminar in May of 1996, we decided to address multiculturalism in the context of national unity. The moderator, Amelita Armit, made the case for the need to openly address all the current controversies. Her introduction to the seminar is included in this book, as she weaves together the illustrious life of the late Juliet Cuenco, who dedicated so much of her time to the advancement of multiculturalism, and the debate around this complex subject matter.

A SIXTIES IDEA

The federal policy began innocuously in 1971, perhaps as an overdue sixties idea combined with the need for the federal government, as some charge, to buy the support of the ethnic minorities for bilingualism, and to gain their electoral support. On both scores it was probably successful. Much is made of these crass political motives, but then politics is the stuff of most government policies. Pierre Trudeau's perspective was that if the state respects people for who they are, they in turn will be loyal to the state.

At no time was the proof of this more evident than on the night of October 30, 1996, when Quebec premier Jacques Parizeau laid blame on the "ethnic vote" for the loss of the referendum. Quebec residents of minority ethnic origins remained loyal to Canada in large part because they perceive it as accommodating and accepting of their cultural identity. Critics often balk at this view. They argue instead that multiculturalism fragments Canadian society and makes it less cohesive by creating too much diversity. If this were true, why have ethnic minorities not embraced a separate Quebec? Standing up for Canada in Quebec is not an easy thing to do, especially for a newcomer. It would be easier for immigrants to throw their lot in with the sovereigntists, and get in on the formation of a new country at the ground level. For all the criticism that is directed against multiculturalism, it did not cause the disloyalty that was expected. Rather, the symbolism of respect, equality, tolerance and accommodation conveyed by multiculturalism has created a high degree of loyalty to the federal state.

For those who remain unconvinced, we draw attention to the words of Louise Harel who was appointed Minister for Cultural Communities and Immigration a few days after the referendum. She stated the Parti Québécois had to build better relations with minorities, noting that this had been difficult in the past "because of the ravages of multiculturalism".

The issues of loyalty and Canadian identity are addressed in articles by members of the five political parties represented in Parliament. These include MPs Hedy Fry of the Liberal Party (the federal Secretary of State for Multiculturalism), Christiane Gagnon of the Bloc Québécois, Cliff Breitkreuz of the Reform Party, and Simon de Jong of the NDP. There is an essay from senior Progressive Conservative Senator Noël Kinsella. Former Reform Party member (and now a member of the Progressive Conservative Party) MP Jan Brown also provides her perspective, as did Liberal MP Jean Augustine. These essays clearly describe the divergent views on multiculturalism that are contained that are contained in the Parliament of Canada.

Joseph Wong and Elliot Tepper argue that multiculturalism was really a matter of recognizing full and equal citizenship in a pluralistic society. Irving Abella has covered this matter from an international and Canadian Jewish perspective. Gabrielle Nishiguchi argues that the "hyphenated" concept can undermine Canadian identity.

More than fostering the retention of foreign cultures, the federal policy and numerous provincial programs encourage ethnic groups to achieve greater social cohesion and mutual respect by promoting intergroup relations. Lilian To addresses the "Canadianness" of multiculturalism with a particular focus on British Columbia, and insists that we do not have an option about this policy. It simply addresses a demographic and social reality.

Over the years, some critics have alleged that the multiculturalism policy was a deliberate scheme to allow the state to monitor the activities of ethnic groups; further, that it sought to placate community leaders and stave off their demands for more serious action. There is evidence to suggest that program funds have been used to encourage community leaders and organizations to be more sympathetic to the government in power. This kind of favouritism is also present in other spheres of government which aim to influence the direction of interest groups. There is no question that the policy has been misused from time to time, but that is little reason to abandon it. Rather, it suggests a need to tighten up the procedures for administering programs and funds.

In her essay, Amy Go argues that the policy was always minimal and never very successful. Yet, she finds herself in the uncomfortable position of defending it only because the neo-conservative attack is so overwhelming and there is a need to protect whatever little there is. In a similar vein, the NDP's Simon de Jong decries the federal government's acquiescence to this pressure.

Like most aspects of public policy, multiculturalism has grown and matured with time. Song and dance and the endless multicultural festivals were the necessary visible beginnings of the policy. Various contributors allude to the economic benefits that multiculturalism has brought us and how some of these cultural expressions have become internationally recognized tourist attractions. The promotion of heritage languages and cultures has given us a valuable human capital asset. For example, many of the Canadians who are forging trade links with emerging economies in areas like Asia and eastern Europe have origins in those parts of the world, an issue that Jonathan Calof has eloquently addressed.

Today, the issues being addressed, whether in government, business, media or the voluntary sector, centre on organizational change, equality, race relations, social justice and the evolving Canadian identity. Lloyd Stanford and Andrew Cardozo address some of the historical issues around multiculturalism, bilingualism and national unity.

Li Zong and Fo Niemi look at some of the key issues around racism and the new directions multiculturalism is moving in.

NETWORK OF POLICIES

There is an array of federal legislation that complements the Multiculturalism Policy. The most important is the Canadian Charter of Rights and Freedoms and the specific sections that give recognition to the multicultural heritage of Canadians, guarantee freedom of religion, and disallow discrimination based on race, national or ethnic origin, colour, and religion.

There is also the Canadian Human Rights Act, the Employment Equity Act, and criminal laws that address hate groups and propaganda. In his essay, Emilio Binavince looks at various aspects of the legal framework and the role that ethnic minorities can play in building national unity.

What is most often overlooked by supporters and critics alike is that the Mulroney government's Canadian Multiculturalism Act of 1988 obligated all federal departments and agencies to implement multiculturalism as it applies to their mandates. Hence it addresses matters such as justice, the status of women, broadcasting, health policy, museums, small business and international trade. To some, this is a tremendous opportunity; to others a massive and needless burden. Some of the essays by the political representatives and other writers present their views on the implications of the federal act.

Canada has changed since the Multiculturalism Policy came into effect 25 years ago. We have all heard the stories of how immigrants were made to feel embarrassed and ashamed of their different cultures, names, accents, foods and clothes. This was most difficult for immigrant children in schools. When multiculturalism got underway in the seventies its slogan was “celebrating our differences”. For a time, this campaign was quite successful. It embodied our commitment to mutual respect, tolerance and accommodation. It said to all Canadians that we should celebrate our cultural traditions and not be ashamed of our differences.

Somewhere along the way, the message this slogan conveyed changed. Celebrating our multiculturalism heritage came to be interpreted as an assertion that we had little in common to bind us together and were divided by our differences. There is now a feeling in some quarters that attempts to accommodate minorities have resulted in a loss of traditional Canadian identity and customs. Examples often cited include the wearing of the turban in the RCMP and Legion Halls, and the hostile accusations of racism at Nellie's shelter for women, which forced the resignation of founder June Callwood.

People who espouse this view often believe in the liberal commitment to the primacy of the individual. They perceive a conflict between individual and collective rights, and generally disapprove of state-funded activities that promote culture of any kind. They see this as best handled by individuals. Essays by Independent MP Jan Brown and Reform MP Cliff Breitkreuz approach the topic from this perspective. English teacher Nathan Greenfield is especially critical of what he sees as the use of race by government to address systemic discrimination.

Multiculturalism has many critics, but most Canadians see it as an important defining symbol of our identity. A review of public opinion data by Louis Musto reveals that there is majority public support for the aims of the federal multiculturalism programs, especially those that work to eliminate racism and racial discrimination, overcome problems of integration faced by ethnocultural minorities, and promote our shared values.

ABANDON WHAT?

If the federal government abandoned multiculturalism tomorrow, racial and cultural tensions would remain. This reality is not the result of the policy. Indeed, the policy creates a context within which to address these issues. For all their fire and brimstone, the critics have yet to define a viable alternative.

After 25 years, it is important to offer proof that the Multiculturalism Policy and the force of its symbolism have been successful. The following are examples of outcomes of the federal policy, most of which have moved beyond its purview:

- There is a society-wide acceptance that we live in a diverse society which is to be valued.
- Awareness of cultural diversity is reflected in school curricula.
- Multicultural sensitivity is shown by teachers and counselors in schools, daycare and community centres.
- Numerous minority writers have enriched the world of "Can Lit" such as Josef Svorecky, Michael Ondaatje, Rohinton Mistry, Denise Chong, M.G. Vassanji, Skye Lee, Neil Bissoondath and Nino Ricci.
- The media have made progress towards faïrer portrayal and more inclusion of minorities in their ranks.
- Advertisers are much better at including minorities in advertising.

- Business establishments have made progress in removing systemic barriers faced by members of ethnic minority groups.
- Hate propaganda laws have been passed.
- Police forces have implemented race relations training.
- The Canada Council has supported several minority artists, writers and art forms.
- Political parties are making more efforts to recruit a wider set of candidates.

Despite this progress, change has been painfully slow. There is still lots to be done, and in recent years a vocal backlash has stalled much of the progress. Nevertheless, we have dealt with our diversity better than most other countries. Canada is respected around the world for the way it has managed to do this. It does not make sense to turn back now. Geoffrey Pearson shares his views on building cultural peace in Canada from the perspective of his experience in various countries. Karim H. Karim has documented how policies of diversity are handled in various other countries, namely Australia, the United States and the United Kingdom.

FEDERAL REVIEW

In October of 1996, the federal government announced a renewed multiculturalism program that would build a more inclusive and cohesive society by addressing three objectives: "social justice, identity and civic participation". It would seem that the underlying theme can be summed up in one word, "integration". This concept falls somewhere between the two extremes of forced assimilation and planned segregation. The aim is to integrate all cultures in Canada so that we may evolve into a unique Canadian blend that respects our history, includes our present, and is open to our future.

A government-wide commitment is needed to address racism, advance the integration of newcomers and increase respect and understanding among all Canadians. A range of federal departments and institutions, including the Justice and Solicitor General departments and the RCMP, have been addressing some of these issues for years. A formal network of these federal institutions would be useful to co-ordinate efforts to combat racism.

Jonathan Calof looks at the need to better utilize our diversity to advance our trade and export potential. Perhaps it is time for the International Trade department to set up a special "Canadian Diversity and Trade Branch" with the specific mandate of linking businesses with ethnocultural community organizations and immigrant groups that are knowledgeable in trade matters. On a related issue, Jean Augustine argues that our cultural and linguistic diversity give us an advantage in getting involved with the Information Highway.

Aggressive work is needed to advance multiculturalism, harmonious race relations, and equality in employment. Most of all, the government and, more to the point, Canadians must make their supportive voices heard if they want the policy and the ideal it represents to stand the test of time. Policies which face much public attack and receive little public defence soon whither. The next few years will determine whether the defenders or the critics will win the battle over multiculturalism.

This book is the first of three volumes that will address multiculturalism and Canadian identity. It is our hope that these works will initiate further debate on a topic that is likely to be prominent on the public agenda in the years ahead.

ALL OVER THE MAP: THE LACK OF CONSENSUS ON CANADIAN UNITY

Andrew Cardozo

On the one hand, Canadians say we want very fundamental changes to our federation, while on the other, we will only allow our politicians to make incremental modifications. This is primarily because there is little consensus on what these changes should be.

The debate about multiculturalism is perhaps only a symptom of our national malaise. We really cannot come to a clear consensus on multiculturalism until there is consensus about our basic values and the definition of Canada. It is unfortunate though, that some critics of multiculturalism insist that we should act in reverse order—abolish multiculturalism and the solutions to our national unity problems will instantly appear.

If the differences or the problems are very large and we allow only step by step solutions, then it means that we will take a very long time to get the job done. The quest for national unity has been with us for a long time, since well before Confederation, and will be with us for a long time. It is this inherent contradiction—the big problems and small solutions dichotomy—which accounts for this never ending debate. To some, this is the Canadian curse; to others it is the Canadian blessing. For me it is a blessing. What better country to live in than one that so openly and constantly evaluates and re-evaluates itself. It is, after all, a discourse that allows us to continually address and update our national identity, our common goals, and our shared purpose.

We are, however, not alone in this quest for national identity. The debate is raging in just about every other country in the world, whether we look at the United States, Russia, Great Britain, Italy, Israel, the former Yugoslavia, Northern Ireland, India or Algeria. We are just more experienced at it.

As we get closer together (thanks to travel, phone and fax lines, the news media, and now the Internet), we seem to become more concerned about our group identities. We are struggling to maintain our differences and our values. Author Michael Ignatieff has called this a "narcissism of minor difference".[1] Unfortunately, it is not only that we struggle to maintain our own identities, but there seems to be a feeling that one can only survive if someone else can be undermined. So the quest for cultural maintenance involves not only maintaining one's own culture, but trying to subvert someone else's. This is how cultural maintenance turns into prejudice, then into discrimination, then into racism and then into hate. This is why the understandable cause of cultural maintenance has to be monitored to make sure the positive benefits do not turn into negative currents. Ensuring that these energies are used creatively and not destructively is a constant challenge.

The excitement about the "global village" that Marshall MacLuhan talked about three decades ago has worn off. Today the global village is coming true in volumes but has become too domineering and terrifying for many of us.

I would like to examine the differences and similarities in the context of the Canadian debate on national unity by addressing the following three questions:

- What is Canada?
- What is the role of government?

- What are the core principles of our society?

WHAT IS CANADA?

There remains remarkably little consensus about the definition of the country, and this lack of consensus goes back to Confederation. There are at least five major points of view on Canada which are all separate from each other.

Canada as a country of ten equal provinces

For many in English speaking Canada, the country is made up of ten equal provinces, each of which occupy the same importance and operate under generally similar systems. Quebec is therefore just one of ten, just like the others.[2]

Canada as a country of two founding peoples

In this view, the two founding peoples are those of British and French origin. What is interesting is that the delegates to the Charlottetown Conference of 1864, who developed the basic constitution of Canada, had different versions of the outcome of the meeting—and no one took minutes. The English-speaking provinces saw it as an agreement that Canada would consist of five equal provinces (Ontario, Quebec, Prince Edward Island, New Brunswick and Nova Scotia). Quebec saw it as a partnership between two founding peoples, and this view remains very evident in Quebec.

Today, an updated version is that Quebec is one nation which is pluri-ethnic, with a predominant French language and culture, while the English speaking provinces form the other nation.

From this perspective it can be seen why the "distinct society"[3] recognition was such a good compromise, as it recognized the unique composition that Quebec believes itself to be, but did not try to tell the other provinces that they constituted a separate monolithic identity.

Canada as a country of English origin

This version suggests that Canada is primarily of British origin and English speaking. Quebec and the French language are somehow included, but not in a terribly important manner. Bilingualism and multiculturalism are dismissed as “politically correct” liberal polices that are undermining the country.[4] Some who feel this way seldom give much credit to the British tradition and see themselves as the ultimate Canadians with no homage paid to other countries.

Canada as a country of three nations

This perspective suggests that Canada consists of three nations: English speaking, French speaking and Aboriginal. There is a progressive perspective which says that each of the three are characterized by diversity, i.e. recognizing the diversity among Aboriginal peoples and even among First Nations (Indian people); and the diversity that exists within each linguistic group.[5] A more conservative notion says that ethnic minorities can choose which nation they would assimilate into.[6] The role of the provinces is not so important.

Canada as a country with a foundation of four pillars

According to this version, the Canadian community consists of four ethnocultural pillars: English (or Anglo-Celtic), French, Aboriginal, and the other ethnic minorities combined as a fourth pillar. While all Canadians live in an integrated manner, the differences would be recognized in a positive way. Again, the role of the provinces is not important.

WHAT IS THE ROLE OF GOVERNMENT?

The debate over the role of government has become more pronounced in recent years. These days, there are two basic viewpoints in the general political spectrum. It would appear that we are teetering between these two models, having dismissed all others as undesired or unaffordable.

Moderately activist government

There are those who believe that government should play an activist role as a regulator and equalizer in various areas: economic, social, cultural, environmental, etc. Indeed, the government of Canada does play a role in all these areas although it is in a phase of program review[7] designed to reduce government costs by reassessing what it does.

The government regulates society in many areas such as trade and tariff policies, fiscal policy, waste disposal, the criminal code, human rights codes, bilingual services, health services and broadcasting policy. It provides direct assistance to citizens in various areas such as family assistance and pensions, and controls some policies such as immigration, customs and correctional services.

In many cases, the government provides regulation or direct services for the benefit of some. There are those who believe that such regulations should not exist. Take, for example, the regulations that prevent banks from selling insurance: Banks want the government to drop such regulations, while the insurance industry insists the government must maintain them.

In many areas, the federal government has developed a shared jurisdiction with provinces. While the Constitution has spelled out the division of powers in most areas, it also provides for shared jurisdiction in others. By offering financial assistance in recent decades though, the federal government has also entered into areas originally defined as only provincial jurisdiction.

Drastically reduced government

The opinion that government should be drastically reduced in size and function has been around for a long time. This view has gained considerable support in this decade, most notably since the rise of conservatism in Great Britain, the United States and New Zealand. In Canada, this viewpoint has been championed by the Reform Party federally and by the Progressive Conservative governments in Alberta, Manitoba and Ontario. This perspective generally calls for a federal government that would do little more than address matters of law and order (and, even that, as directed by the provinces), defense and international affairs. Most other areas are best left in the hands of provincial governments which are "closer to the people" and which can better respond to the particular needs of the residents in the province.

The viewpoint that we need more interventionist governments appears to be quite out of favour these days—except when some specific issues are discussed such as law and order.

CORE PRINCIPLES

Canadians tend to identify core principles of our society as democracy, the rule of law, justice, equality, respect for differences, bilingualism and multiculturalism. But on each of these, we are divided as to how far to go. There is also an agenda that deals with caring in our society; proponents of this agenda are protective of universal health care, social services, free school education, and care for the elderly through pensions.[8]

The debates on justice and equality are endless: Does equality actually exist because the Constitution says we are all equal? Or, do we need policies to bring about equality—policies such as employment equity, human rights codes, status of women policies, Aboriginal self government, bilingualism and multiculturalism? On each of these tools for equality and caring there is active debate these days.

There is disagreement over what is meant by the rule of law. For example, some of us believe that this includes limiting the sale and ownership of guns, while others believe that gun control is not the answer to crime and in fact denies democratic rights. Another case in point concerns our duties as taxpayers. Recently, two senior members of the Ontario government said it was quite normal for businesses to avoid paying taxes whereas cheating by welfare recipients was not to be tolerated.

Much as we respect democracy, our elected government and House of Commons can be overruled by the unelected Senate and unelected Governor General, not to mention the Queen, our unelected, titular head of state. Attempts to have an elected Senate have repeatedly failed, and there has been no serious attempt to replace the Monarchy, and its representative in Canada, the Governor General, with an elected officer. Further, the appointed judiciary has the ability to overturn the decisions of the Parliament if they determine that the laws passed violate the Constitution. And, again, there is debate on whether this is, in fact, the case, given that the constitution they are interpreting was created by elected officials, and whether the very purpose of a constitution is to keep the legislators in line.

Nevertheless, it is fair to say that while these unelected bodies can overrule the elected chamber, for the most part, the will of the elected body has prevailed.

Similarly, bilingualism and multiculturalism enjoy considerable public support. While there is debate on their appropriateness, there are three viewpoints on both: that the current policies are about right; that they do not go far enough; and that they go too far.

The erosion of core principles

With each of our core principles under active debate, we can only say that we have common core principles in a very general way.

It is worth pointing out that many of these core principles are not uniquely Canadian, and are in fact quite universal. Ironically, principles that are under attack by the more conservative elements in our society are the ones that are either uniquely Canadian or at least not very common, such as multiculturalism and bilingualism, welfare policies, universal health care and pensions.

The greatest threat to who we are as a country and the Canadian core principles has come from the strong belief that we need less government. This is both a Canadian neo-conservative viewpoint and one that is influenced by conservatives in the United States. Many of our core principles cost money—money that we have been willing to pay in our taxes for several decades. Now, however, there is a belief that this can no longer be done.

It is disturbing that we tend to blame the wrong people for the erosion of the Canadian identity and the Canadian standard of living. We blame immigrants and minorities for not adjusting to the Canadian way of living, when in fact they came here precisely because of the Canadian way of life and they actively uphold it. We blame welfare recipients for being on welfare when most of them would love to have jobs if only jobs could be found.

THE MULTICULTURALISM DEBATE

To come back to the debate about multiculturalism, it seems that we will not be able to resolve the areas of difference until we can reach a conclusion on how we define Canada, how we define the role of government and our core principles.

In the meantime, the endless flailing away at multiculturalism can only be seen as a way to vent our collective frustrations at the larger questions which are so much harder to tackle.

This essay was developed from a speech given in August 1996 to the Ulyssean Society at Hart House, University of Toronto.

NOTES

[1] Ignatieff, Michael. "The Narcissism of Minor Difference." *Clash of Identities.* Toronto:Prentice-Hall, 1996.

[2] The Constitution does in fact recognize ten provinces with provincial governments which have similar powers regardless of their size. Each province's influence in the federation though, is different, determined to some extent on population and hence, the number of seats in the House of Commons.

[3] Both the Meech Lake and Charlottetown Accords included a recognition of Quebec as a "distinct society" within Canada. Both accords failed to pass into law.

[4] This view is widely held in some parts of English-speaking Canada, more so the further west you get from Quebec. It was articulated several

decades ago by R.B. Bennett, Prime Minister of Canada. *Debates*. House of Commons. June 7, 1928, p. 3926.

5 This view was put forward by the Council of Canadians prior to the Charlottetown Accord.

6 Best expressed by former newspaper editor, G. Hamilton Southam. "Three distinct societies should be recognized." Letter to the editor, *Ottawa Citizen,* September 23, 1996.

7 Swimmer, Gene. ed. *How Ottawa Spends 1996: Life Under the Knife.* Ottawa: Carleton University Press, 1996. The volume is dedicated to examining the cause and effects of the policy review underway.

8 Peters, Suzanne. *Exploring Canadian Values: Foundations for Well-Being.* Ottawa: Canadian Policy Research Network, Inc., 1995.

REFERENCES

Peters, Suzanne. *Exploring Canadian Values: Foundations for Well-Being.* Canadian Policy Research Networks Inc., 1995.

Annual Report 1994-95 on the Operation of the Multiculturalism Act. Department of Canadian Heritage.

PUBLIC OPINION ON MULTICULTURALISM AND CANADIAN IDENTITY

Louis Musto

Multiculturalism is a concept that is not well understood. This is most evident when its merits are debated. The discussion is often abstract, ambiguous, narrowly focused, and laden with myths and stereotypes.

Many individuals who contribute to the intellectual debate on the subject have a poor understanding of the federal multiculturalism policy. This is also true of the general public. Canadians associate the term with cultural diversity, but they are not fully aware of other aspects of multiculturalism. They do, however, support its different dimensions. The public perspective is at variance with the views espoused by the critics of multiculturalism.

A review of public opinion suggests that multiculturalism has the potential to become a very salient symbol of Canadian identity. The challenge is to present it as more than a recognition of the country's cultural diversity. It should be positioned as an overarching vision of Canada that reflects our sense of tolerance, respect, social justice and civility.

PERCEPTION OF MULTICULTURALISM

Canadians perceive the term multiculturalism as describing a demographic reality. It is associated with cultural diversity, rather than as a government policy or program. See Table 1.

Table 1

Perceptions of Multiculturalism

	% response
A reflection of diversity in society	70
A government policy or program	25
Both	4
Neither	1

Question: Are you more likely to think of multiculturalism as...

(Source: Ekos Research Associates Inc., 1995)

RECOGNITION OF THE FEDERAL MULTICULTURALISM POLICY

About 66% of Canadians recognize that the federal government has a multiculturalism policy. Of these people, six in ten (62%) approve of the federal policy. Overall public support for the policy declined between 1989 and 1995 (Environics Research Group, 1995). The decline can largely be explained by a rise in economic insecurity during the first half of this decade. The difficult economic climate likely diminished tolerance for diversity and change. During this period, for example, there was also public unease over immigration.

Familiarity with the federal multiculturalism policy is low. About 18% of Canadians are extremely (2%) and quite (16%) familiar with the policy. One-third (33%) are somewhat familiar, and almost half (48%) are not at all familiar. (Ekos Research Associates, 1995).

PREFERRED DIRECTION OF THE FEDERAL MULTICULTURALISM POLICY

Criticism of the multiculturalism policy has escalated in recent years. Yet, while Canadians have little awareness and understanding of the federal multiculturalism policy, they are supportive of its objectives and overall direction. Table 2 reveals the strongest support is for actions to educate new Canadians about our common values, laws and institutions (89%); eliminating racism in our institutions (85%); and promoting tolerance (83%). Support is solid for measures that help individuals integrate into mainstream society (79%). Increasingly, the federal multiculturalism policy has moved in this direction since its inception 25 years ago, despite the mythology to the contrary.

There is less endorsement, although majority support, for actions that seek to preserve the cultures of minority groups (55% support). Many likely see this as an individual rather than a government responsibility. Indeed, this is often a major criticism of the federal policy. There is, however, considerable approval for the federal government to promote awareness that cultural and racial diversity is a fundamental characteristic of Canadian society (69%), and of the value of cultural diversity (67%).

Table 2

Preferred Elements of Federal Multiculturalism Programs

	% support
Helping new Canadians learn about Canadian values, laws and institutions	89
Eliminating racism in areas such as health care, justice and education	85
Promoting tolerance through public communications and public education	83
Helping individuals from ethnic and racial minorities integrate into Canadian economic, cultural, political, and social life	79
Helping people integrate into society without having to give up their ethnic identity completely	74
Promoting an awareness that cultural and racial diversity is a fundamental characteristic of Canadian society	69
Promoting the value of cultural diversity	67
Helping health and social services be more accessible to ethnic and racial minorities	64
Helping ethnic minorities in the preservation of their culture	55

Question: Please indicate whether you would support or oppose each of the following elements of federal multiculturalism programs...

(Source: Ekos Research Associates Inc., 1995)

An often heard criticism of multiculturalism is that it will fragment the nation by creating independent cultural systems. Canadians, however, appear to see room for compromise and accommodation on the matter of cultural preservation. They expect newcomers to adapt and adjust to Canadian ways, but they also see a need for acceptance and promotion of cultural differences that do not conflict with the ethos of the larger society. To this end, they strongly endorse public policy that helps people integrate into society without having to completely give up their ethnic identity (74% support).

Public support for cultural diversity bound by commonality is also reflected in a 1995 survey conducted by Decima Research for the Canadian Council of Christians and Jews. Three-quarters (74%) of Canadians agreed that an ideal society is one where "members of the community observe different religions and come from different racial or ethnic backgrounds, but who share a common way of life and common values."

MULTICULTURALISM AS A NATIONAL SYMBOL

Table 3 shows that about seven in ten Canadians believe multiculturalism is an important symbol of national identity. It is not positioned as highly as other symbols, but it nevertheless ranks *above* bilingualism, hockey and the Queen.

Multiculturalism can become a more prominent feature of our national identity by linking it to other dominant symbols. For example, it promotes the values and principles of equality, freedom and justice incorporated in the Canadian Charter of Rights and Freedoms.

SUMMARY

Canadians perceive multiculturalism as a reflection of cultural diversity rather than a government policy. They have little awareness and knowledge of the federal policy, but they generally endorse its objectives. There is public support for government assistance to encourage cultural diversity, although this is perceived as less important than measures that aim to eliminate racism, overcome problems of

Table 3

Symbols of Canadian Unity
(very and somewhat important)

	% response
Canada's health care system	96
National parks	92
Historic Sites	91
The Charter of Rights and Freedoms	90
The Canadian Flag	86
The National Anthem	85
Olympic athletes	84
Canadian literature and music	83
The RCMP	83
Canadian theatre and films	77
Multiculturalism	71
The CBC	68
Bilingualism	65
Hockey	60
The Queen	35

Question: How important are the following to the Canadian identity: very important, somewhat important, not very important, or not at all important?

(Source: Environics Research Group Limited, 1996)

integration faced by ethnocultural and visible minorities, and promote tolerance and shared values. Multiculturalism is viewed by many as one of the touchstones of Canadian identity. Its importance to the overall fabric of the nation can be strengthened by presenting it as an embodiment of our core values of tolerance, respect, justice, and fairness.

This public opinion data also suggests that there is room for the federal government to take a stronger stand in defending and promoting multiculturalism.

The public opinion data in this article was used with permission from Ekos Research Inc., the Environics Research Group Limited, Decima Research, and the Canadian Council of Christians and Jews. The surveys were based on a representative sample of the Canadian population.

PARLIAMENTARY VIEWS ON NATION BUILDING

LIBERAL PARTY: A CONTINUED COMMITMENT TO THE IDEALS OF MULTICULTURALISM

Hedy Fry

In 1996, Canadians marked the 25th anniversary of Canada's becoming the first nation to adopt a multiculturalism policy—a policy that has helped bring us international recognition and opportunity. It has also brought variety, innovation, choice and growth—culturally, socially and economically—while enhancing and promoting our shared Canadian values of fairness, justice and mutual respect.

But a policy, no matter how noble, can only succeed if it is nourished by determined human beings. It is the Canadian people who play such an essential part in ensuring that multiculturalism is and always will be a fundamental characteristic of our flourishing democratic society.

As a physician, I am committed to examining all the facts, doing a thorough check-up and making a considered diagnosis and prognosis. I can say definitively that multiculturalism is thriving. It is true that multiculturalism could use some lifestyle improvements, but the prognosis is for long term health and vitality.

As a physician, I am also always on the lookout for those who would drum up anxieties by spreading misinformation about non-existent problems. In my time as president of British Columbia's Medical Association, I too often saw those who tried to practice medicine without a licence and those who tried to profit on people's concerns by peddling unnecessary, costly and useless treatments. They just don't get it. There are some well-placed people in our country who are spreading misinformation about multiculturalism. There are Canadians in positions of trust who are stirring up needless fears and prescribing harmful prescriptions for multiculturalism.

I am appalled when I hear talk of moving "ethnics" to the back of the shop. I am angered when I hear multiculturalism falsely blamed for creating divisions, and I am infuriated when I hear talk of multiculturalism as harmful to the success of our country. There are elected officials who say they don't oppose multiculturalism, they just don't want it to be part of our law, and there are commentators who say they don't oppose multiculturalism, they just don't want it to be part of our national policy. There are those who say they don't oppose multiculturalism, they just don't want it as part of the Charter of Rights and Freedoms, and there are those who say it is all right to express your cultural identity in your own home but please avoid being multicultural in public.

I believe those elected officials and commentators are wrong. They just don't get it, and they make no effort to understand it. They don't understand the enormous benefits which multiculturalism brings to our country, and they ignore the fact that, as poll after poll shows, Canadians overwhelmingly regard multiculturalism as one of the great selling points of Canada. They don't appreciate that multiculturalism is a hallmark of who we are as a country and what we are as a society.

Multiculturalism is the polar opposite of apartheid. We are not going to go to the back of the shop and then to the back of the bus and then to separate accommodations. We are going to go forward together.

Multiculturalism is the Canadian reality. It is an underpinning of our common values. It is central to our unity and to our identity as Canadians and it is central to Prime Minister Jean Chrétien's philosophical, practical and personal vision of our country.

The criticisms levelled by a few political opponents of multiculturalism are really just the proof of its success. It's because multiculturalism has gone mainstream, it's because ethnocultural groups are making progress that we hear from the far right wing. It is because multiculturalism is more than tokenism that we hear from those who are afraid to open up society, afraid to adapt, afraid to move forward, afraid to build a world respected multicultural future.

As Newfoundland's former Premier Joey Smallwood put it: "I chose Canada." I came to Canada because I wanted to be part of a just society. I wanted to be part of it and I wanted my kids and grandchildren to grow up in it. I wanted to contribute to the building of a nation where national, community and individual identity are all respected; a country where the growth of one society and one people need not limit the growth of the individual or the value of the group; a country which builds its identity collectively while respecting and honouring the distinctness and diversity of its many parts.

The beauty of Canada lies in its geographic, human, linguistic and cultural diversity. That beauty also lies in the fact that our identity which is rooted in our history is still being shaped and all Canadians are part of that great endeavour.

INCLUSION, RESPECT AND PARTICIPATION

Multiculturalism has always been a building block for Canadian society. It is at the heart of the development of a social and economic union based on common values. It is because multiculturalism is such an undeniable characteristic of our country that it has such a critical role in defining our identity for the 21st century.

When we talk about the elimination of systemic barriers, we are really talking about Canada's commitment to inclusion. When we talk about culturally sensitive services, we are really talking about respect. When we talk about multiculturalism, we are really talking about the full and equal participation of Canadians of all backgrounds in the evolution of a dynamic and unified nation.

In my consultations with Canadians I have been told that the types of programming directions that were attractive to ethnocultural communities were those that address the broad societal issues of concern to all Canadians. A pressing concern has been regarding Canadian young people. Canadians are frankly worried about intergenerational problems, equality issues, language barriers, discrimination and barriers to integration.

I have been told that federal multicultural activities should centre on public education, special projects for specific needs, access to services and proactive initiatives by issue based coalitions. I couldn't agree more with all of these points.

The Strategic Review of Multiculturalism which has been underway for the past year is focussed on meeting the changing needs of society. It is focussed on making certain that multiculturalism programs are relevant to the needs of 1996 and the future, and on modernizing our programs and making them more responsive, coordinated and innovative.

We are not reviewing the Multiculturalism Policy of 1971 nor the Canadian Multiculturalism Act of 1988. Their precepts remain relevant and central to what the Program does. We are seeking to keep our programming—the tools that give life to the Policy and Act—apace with

Canada's multicultural reality. We are seeking to break down the ghettoization of multiculturalism. We are seeking an end to the piecemeal approach and an emphasis on the partnership approach—within and across governments, within and across communities within and across institutions.

We all need to reach out within our own spheres of influence and we need to effect social change through a broader community of interest.

In launching the review of the Multiculturalism Program, the government undertook evaluations of what works and what doesn't work. We examined the changing demographics of Canada in detail, studied all the previous research, and did new domestic and comparative research. We looked honestly at the problems and at the even more promising potential.

When I assumed my job as Secretary of State at the end of January, 1996, I considered carefully the suggestions I heard from Canadians that they want to get on with the job of achieving full equality, promoting multiculturalism as an asset to Canada and developing opportunities to advance as citizens within a fully integrated, pluralistic society.

It was suggested that the review process should allow for input by the general public. We have done that and we have heard that Canadians are supportive of multiculturalism as a social fact in Canada. They worry, however, that the general public is not sufficiently aware of or involved in initiatives supported by the Multiculturalism Program. That is a challenge for me and that is a challenge for all organizations promoting the ideals of multiculturalism.

In particular, young Canadians are exceptionally supportive of multiculturalism but they wonder how they fit into our organizational structures, how they can play a larger role in decision-making within communities, within government and across society. That, too, is a major challenge for me and for you.

It was also suggested that the funding criteria of the Multiculturalism Program should focus on the issue being addressed rather than the identity of the applicant group. In my judgment that rings true. Support from the Multiculturalism Program must be based on what you do—not who you are.

Public opinion clearly shows that the principles of multiculturalism are relevant to the Canadian public and supported by the Canadian public. Our programs and our multicultural organizations must reflect that. The principles of multiculturalism are especially relevant to young Canadians and especially supported by them. This is clearly a future-oriented policy. Our programs and our multicultural organizations must reflect that also.

I am a realist about the important issues facing multiculturalism. I am also an extraordinary optimist. Most Canadians support the need to incorporate multiculturalism issues across government departments, across all levels of government and across the range of public and private sector institutions in Canada. They want to address the barriers that impede the achievement of equality and full participation of all communities and citizens in Canadian society. They want to improve public understanding of multiculturalism and its advantages for Canada and to build on those advantages. The achievement of these ends will not come by miracles and it will not come overnight. It will require Canadians to speak out loudly, forcefully and vigorously for who we are as Canadians and where we want to go together. It will oblige us to make choices, set priorities and engage in an ongoing dialogue among ourselves and with all Canadians.

The federal government must lead and we will lead. But like-minded groups and individuals have an instrumental part to play in bringing all Canadians into the multiculturalism fold, in reaching out to Canadians and in bringing people together.

Building a nation is a dynamic process. Building our Canadian identity is an organic process. Changing the country for the better means building partnerships. Appealing to the better side of human nature means opening up to others. Encouraging respect means encouraging inclusion. These are the challenges we share together and this is the path we are going to blaze together.

This essay is developed from a speech given at the Juliet Cuenco Memorial Seminar on May 27, 1996, Ottawa.

BLOC QUÉBÉCOIS: INTEGRATION RATHER THAN MULTICULTURALISM

Christiane Gagnon

The position of the Bloc Québécois is very clear on the federal government's multiculturalism policy. We believe there are several reasons why this policy should be abolished.

To put this debate into perspective, it would be useful to consider the official definition of this multiculturalism policy as read in a news bulletin from the Library of Parliament. We read that the term multiculturalism in Canada evokes the presence and survival of various racial and ethnic minorities that identify themselves as being different and wish to stay that way.

We should now look at the sequence of events that led up to the adoption of the policy on multiculturalism. It was adopted in 1971 under the Trudeau government, and the report of the Royal Commission on Bilingualism and Biculturalism had been published. The fourth volume of the report dealt with the contribution of "the other ethnic groups" to the enrichment of Canadian culture and recommended the integration (and not assimilation) into Canadian society of non-founding ethnic groups, recognizing their rights and privileges as citizens and making them equal participants in Canada's institutions.

We should also remember that a new political party, the Parti Québécois, was founded in Quebec with the sovereignty of Quebec as its stated objective, and that in the election held the previous year, it obtained 22 per cent of the popular vote.

How ironic. Feeling the pressure from this new expression of Quebec's desire for independence, coming as it did shortly after the October crisis, the Trudeau team, including the present Prime Minister, decided to make some adjustments to the report's recommendation. As a result, the concept of integration that would recognize the rights of members of ethnic groups and their equal participation in society was abandoned in favour of the concept of promoting cultural differences. In so doing, the whole dialectic of two founding peoples with their own language and culture was submerged and diluted in this ocean of other languages and cultures.

It was a fine sleight of hand, and most Canadians did not notice, except, of course, Quebecers. Through then Premier Robert Bourassa, Quebecers resolutely dissociated themselves from this concept.

In an open letter to Mr. Trudeau, Mr. Bourassa first reminded his federal counterpart that his proposal was a betrayal of the work done by the Commission, whose focus had been bilingualism and biculturalism, and thus the equal status of the two founding peoples. He regretted Mr. Trudeau's decision to dissociate culture and language. He went on to reject out of hand a policy whose objective would be to promote languages other than French in Quebec. Finally, he reminded the federal leader that in this case, the jurisdictions were purely provincial.

Quebec never changed its position, although leaders and political options changed regularly over the years. In fact, Quebec developed its own policy for integrating cultural communities, a policy similar to the one proposed by the Laurendeau-Dunton Royal Commission.

In Quebec, the emphasis is on integration. Not assimilation but integration. The official definition of integration is as follows: integration is a long term multi-dimensional process of adaptation, distinct from assimilation. In this process, the knowledge and use of the common language of Quebec society is a fundamental driving force. The process is consolidated in a society, where participation by all Quebecers is guaranteed and where immigrants and members of cultural communities find their place and are recognized as full members of the communal, social and political life of a pluralistic, francophone society.

This policy received unanimous approval in Quebec; it was never an issue, unlike the Canadian policy.

We cannot help but notice that multiculturalism enjoys anything but unanimous approval. The Decima and Gallup polls published in 1993 showed that 75 per cent of Canadians rejected the policy of multiculturalism and favoured a style of integration similar to Quebec's.

Given the government's investment in multiculturalism, it is a sad thing to see it fail. For the year 1993-94 alone, the government invested $38.846 million. The program has existed for 20 years. How many billions of dollars have been invested to date in a flawed policy which the country does not want?

The policy is not working and even its target public, members of ethnic communities, are criticizing it. I cite as an example the overwhelming support for Neil Bissoondath's book, *Selling Illusions*. His supporters were unanimous in saying that the government should only concern itself with helping immigrants to integrate into our society and fighting racism—end of story. He noted that the federal government's policy tended to create ethnic ghettos, which in no way foster integration and full participation in political, economic and social life.

We also cannot leave unmentioned the absurdities made possible by the multiculturalism policy. Barely six months ago, a consultation paper from the Minister of Justice proposed that culture or religion be permitted as a defence against criminal charges. Because of the ensuing uproar, the Minister had to recant and withdraw the proposal. That is one example of how far some people will go to promote different cultures.

In closing, I would like to stress that a sovereign Quebec would continue to favour integration and respect. The Quebec government has reconfirmed this position recently.

Please allow me to quote the Deputy Premier: “Quebec will not use the public purse to subsidize cultural differences. Our government is against multiculturalism. Although the Quebec government acknowledges the fact that Quebec is multi-ethnic, it favours a policy of cultural convergence in one common culture, fortified by foreign sources.” That sums up well Quebec's position on multiculturalism and deals with the issue effectively.

This essay is developed from a speech given on April 5, 1995 in the House of Commons.

REFORM PARTY: FEDERAL FUNDING FOR MULTICULTURALISM A NEEDLESS EXPENSE

Cliff Breitkreuz

The Reform Party has long been on the record in calling for the withdrawal of federal funding to multicultural groups. However, just because I think the state should not be funding various cultural groups does not mean that I dislike these groups. Just because I disagree with government imposed multicultural policies, it should not be construed to suggest that I dislike other linguistic or ethnic groups. I am arguing against government policy, not against cultural groups.

After all, my roots are different from the roots of many other people. Together, generations of our various ancestors came to this country to settle and build what became, by far, the best country in the world. This country was opened up, settled and built without a multicultural policy. In fact, I doubt if the term "multiculturalism" was even coined when my parents came to this country back in the twenties.

My roots are a mixture—a real hodgepodge so to speak. My linguistic heritage is Prussian German but my ancestral affiliation and connection include not only central European heritage, but east European heritage, Slavic heritage, including Ukrainian, Polish and Russian. My parents understood and spoke these languages, plus what they called Yiddish. I am led to believe that Yiddish is a kind of

Germanic way of speaking Hebrew. I really do not know if that makes any linguistic sense. Who am I to question what makes sense in a land, in a country, that encompasses much of the earth's land mass with over 150 cultural groups. Come to think of it, perhaps there are lessons to be learned given the turmoil that existed for centuries in tsarist imperial Russia, then in the former Soviet Union and presently in the newly created state of Russia.

My parents left their homelands, along with hundreds of thousands of other people, having lived in those lands for almost 200 years. They left to escape the tyranny that was to enslave the people for over 70 years. They came to Canada, where everything was new and very unfamiliar. They had nothing when they came halfway around the world.

However they had freedom. They had liberty. They had liberty and freedom that the people back in the land from whence my parents came could not even imagine or dream about. My parents embraced their newly adopted country with energy and a zeal that was typical of newcomers during that time. Like those who came from places other than Britain, they soon learned English like everyone else. Some youngsters did not learn English until they started school.

For years, for generations, like thousands of families not only from eastern Europe but from all over the world, they held on to some aspects of the culture that they had lived with before they came to this country.

These people usually came with little or no money and they received not one thin dime from government. Not only did they not ask for money, they did not expect any government money. They came to this country for freedom and for the tremendous opportunities that this great and beautiful land afforded them. They settled and built communities that helped to build this country.

I suggest that what transpired during those pioneering decades was real, genuine, unvarnished multiculturalism. All these people, these families from varied backgrounds, from different parts of the world worked together and co-operated to build churches, schools and communities.

That was multiculturalism at its finest, with no government dollars. They were all proud of the fact that they had become and were Canadian.

Since government funding for all types of programs began, many communities have divided. Friction and animosity have developed. Dependency on the state, on government handouts, has been created. Apparently, the previous minister responsible for multiculturalism in the Liberal Government thinks so too because she has recently mused that Canada has no culture.

I would suggest that the elites should leave the confines of Ottawa and visit rural Canada, the West and Atlantic Canada. They might be pleasantly surprised at the flourishing culture. I suspect culture in this country would flourish even more and probably bring Canadians closer together if the state, along with its close sister, multiculturalism, would only get its nasty little nose out of culture.

This essay is taken from a speech given on April 5, 1995 in the House of Commons.

NEW DEMOCRATIC PARTY: STANDING UP FOR OUR VALUES

Simon de Jong

The New Democratic Party has long stood for human rights when it was unpopular to do so. We support policies like multiculturalism and employment equity because we respect diversity and want to advance equality of opportunity. These are essential elements of the Canadian identity and national unity.

Our current political composition is problematic. It does not bode well for this Parliament when one hears the position taken by the Bloc Québécois. The Official Opposition party is so narrowly focused in its own little world that I am afraid it misses the much larger point, the larger reality that most Canadians are living in.

The position of the Reform Party is also most unfortunate for Canada. They suggest we should focus our efforts on the pride in being Canadians. I have always felt that my support of multiculturalism was my way of celebrating being Canadian. One of the major essences of Canada is the fact that we are not a melting pot and that we celebrate our diversity. In this diversity is our strength.

We view Canadian culture as open-ended. It is growing and changing as new immigrants, from many cultures, add to our mix. Both the Bloc and the Reform Parties view Canadian culture as being static—

they want to preserve and cling to what has existed in the past and are afraid of change.

The Liberal government has done little to defend multiculturalism from the endless and unfounded attacks from the Bloc and the Reform Party. Rather, under the guise of financial restraint, the Multiculturalism Program has been whittled down bit by bit since this government took office. Instead of stressing the unifying aspects and mutual respect that multiculturalism facilitates, the government seems to have adopted the belief that diversity is our weakness.

We see the benefits of multiculturalism everywhere. For instance, we see people of Ukrainian, Croatian, Chinese or Vietnamese descent opening up trade connections and possibilities with the countries of their origin. This is a tremendous economic plus for Canada.

When we see throughout history the rise of great nations, those great nations embraced multiculturalism, different thoughts, different traditions and different ideas. This coming together made countries great. I believe that if multiculturalism does its job in Canada it will help make Canada great.

The government must continue the work of the Multiculturalism Program and redirect some of the things the Program is doing. It could be more successful in some areas. The fact that racism is on the rise in these hard economic times is a legitimate and serious concern. Certainly here, the Program has an important task to fulfill.

As we head towards the 21st century, multiculturalism must be focused on fighting racism, advancing equality, facilitating immigrant integration and melding all our cultures into the unique model of Canadian culture. This type of blend, rather than a melting pot, is what will strengthen Canada; this is what should determine policy and expenditure priorities.

IMMIGRATION

The NDP has long believed that Canada is essentially a nation of immigrants. Immigration has made enormous contributions to the success of the Canadian economy over the years, and the mix of people of various ethnic origins has enriched our national life.

From a purely economic standpoint, new Canadians are a major asset to this country. New Canadians establish small businesses, increase demand for consumer goods, and create new jobs. The self employment rate among immigrants is well above the Canadian average, and new immigrants draw less frequently on income assistance programs than Canadian born residents. With their commitment to building a new life in Canada, immigrants are frequently vigorous in their pursuit of opportunities for developing new knowledge and new skills. In addition, many bring with them levels of education and skills which are in short supply domestically. It is a telling statistic that almost half of Canadians holding doctorate degrees were born outside of Canada.

Canada has also benefited culturally from a rich ethnic mix, which has enhanced the variety and diversity of Canadian music, theatre, art, literature, dance and cuisine. To cite examples of the contribution of recent immigrants to Canadian cultural life: in 1994, a new Canadian, Rohinton Mistry, was awarded the coveted Giller and Governor General awards for his novel *Such a Long Journey,* while Michael Ondaatje shared in the Booker Prize for *The English Patient*.

The advantages of an open approach to immigration are reflected in the attitudes and values of Canadian children. In general, Canadian children who are exposed to a wide range of cultural, literary and religious traditions learn respect for and tolerance of ethnic differences, and an appreciation of different cultural strengths and perspectives. The extent to which Canada is regarded internationally as an open, tolerant and egalitarian nation, is at least in part a reflection of our openness to new cultural and ethnic groups. As such, our policies must continue to be driven by open-minded values rather than the narrow-minded views that the present government is picking up from the Reform Party and the Bloc Québécois.

In fact, Canadians are frequently ahead of their governments in this regard. In 1979-80, when the "boat people" from Cambodia were looking for refuge, the Conservative Canadian government said that it would accept 4000 persons as refugees. The New Democrat mayor of Ottawa, Marion Dewar, responded that her city could absorb that many refugees alone, and Ottawans opened their hearts and their doors to a new wave of immigrants. Mayor Dewar's example shamed the federal government into expanding its program for refugee settlement, and at the same time created a much more cosmopolitan environment in our nation's capital.

In recent years, New Democrat MPs have been at the forefront for advancing multiculturalism, immigration and human rights. Former MPs such as Ernie Epp, Dan Heap, Margaret Mitchell and Howard McCurdy did a great deal during their time in Parliament.

In keeping with our belief in the inherent value of immigration in building Canada, New Democrats believe that the right to come here should not be restricted to a select group of wealthy people. We recognize the importance of family in immigrant communities and in Canada as a whole, and believe that the Canadian government must live up to its stated commitment to family reunification by devoting adequate resources to processing the applications of all close family members including all children, and eliminate priority processing of applications based on financial considerations.

We also support an open and humanitarian refugee policy that would allow an oral hearing to all refugee claimants and would admit those who qualify under the Geneva Convention on Refugees, regardless of relations between the refugee producing country and the Canadian and American governments.

Despite the negative rhetoric from the Reform Party and more recently from the Progressive Conservatives, New Democrats remain committed to the view that multiculturalism is a fundamental part of Canada's national character. It is time that the Liberal government took a stronger stand in defending multiculturalism, and even advancing it. They should stand up to the right wing pressures and stand up for Canadian values.

PROGRESSIVE CONSERVATIVE PARTY: GUIDING OUR FUTURE THROUGH AN UNDERSTANDING OF OUR PAST

Noël A. Kinsella

Multiculturalism is a fact of our past and present. It will continue to be a fundamental characteristic of our vision for the future—if we are to have a future. The first Vanier Professor at Trent University, W.L. Morton, wrote that Canada was becoming more and more populist and pluralist and that if "...tradition were not transmitted, the society would perish; only if [tradition] is transmitted from generation to generation can Canada survive."[1]

HISTORICAL PERSPECTIVE

The nation of Canada was built by those who can trace their ancestry to the four corners of the globe, generation after generation. Indeed, Canadian society is a truly global and metropolitan community. While our history books might teach that Canada was founded by the British and the French (nary a mention of the indigenous communities), and while many of our symbols and the model of our system of governance indicates this base, the people of Canada are a great amalgam of many cultures, a great coat of many colours.

Long before the federal government articulated a public policy statement on multiculturalism, the realities of multiculturalism had found expression in legislation and practise. Those multicultural realities have not always been marked by justice and fairness. This was unhappily demonstrated by the treatment, during the first part of this century, of Canadians of Chinese origin vis à vis the "head tax", and the experiences of Canadians of Japanese origin during the 1940s.

Almost fifty years ago, Canada became a signatory to the United Nations Universal Declaration of Human Rights, an instrument which has become the Magna Carta of the twentieth century. As a signatory, Canada recognized the inherent dignity and equality of all peoples. Based on this inspiration, Canada's federal and provincial governments enacted anti-discrimination legislation through the 1950s. In 1960, Prime Minister Diefenbaker's Canadian Bill of Rights was passed by Parliament and this was followed by numerous human rights statutes enacted by the provinces.

The programmatic intervention of the federal government in the promotion of multiculturalism was facilitated by the 1971 policy statement on multiculturalism. The interest of Canadians in the area of ethno-cultural identity increased substantially. It was significant that, during the elaboration of the Canadian Charter of Rights and Freedoms in the early 1980s, the principle which is now enshrined in Section 27 of the Charter was embraced: "This Charter shall be interpreted in a manner consistent with the preservation and enhancement of the multicultural heritage of Canadians."

Later, both the 1988 enactment by Parliament of the Multiculturalism Act and the redress of the wrong perpetrated on Canadians of Japanese origin were hailed by many as major achievements of the Progressive Conservative government. Strangely enough, Prime Minister Mulroney's initiative to establish a specific Department of Multiculturalism and Citizenship received less than enthusiastic support, particularly from some of the major national and regional ethnocultural organizations. For example, the *Congresso Nazionale degli italo canadesi* wrote in a brief that:

> *While the notion of a separate department of multiculturalism may be desirable, some key amendments must be made to the Bill in order to ensure that this new department not enshrine a ghetto for a significant component of the population.*[2]

They were concerned that a separate multiculturalism department would "cause a deterioration...by creating arbitrary distinctions between Canadians of French and British origin and other Canadians." In May 1993, an examination of the concept, development and promotion of Canadian citizenship by the Senate included a recommendation to enact a new Citizenship Act to reflect the pluralist, officially bilingual, and multicultural nature of Canadian society. It also included a recommendation that reflected the thinking of those concerned about "ghettoization": "(t)hat the Department of Multiculturalism and Citizenship be renamed the Department of Citizenship and Multi-ulturalism."[3] Early on in the committee's deliberations it became clear that citizenship was an area of major importance and that it was not receiving adequate attention. Those following the issue learned that Parliamentarians must ensure that our citizenship speaks to all Canadians—native born and naturalized alike. This lesson has been lost in present-day Ottawa.

CURRENT STATUS

Currently, multiculturalism has been downgraded to a programme within the Department of Canadian Heritage. This action seems to have been accepted by the major ethnocultural associations. Some have speculated that the extremist voices in the caucus of the Reform Party and the obstructionist attitudes of the members of the Bloc Québécois corralled the major ethnocultural organizations into accepting the present government's outright diminution of multiculturalism and the decreased level of importance Canadian diversity is to have in terms of the machinery of government.

In some quarters there is a push to have the federal government remove itself from institutional multiculturalism. If, by this, one means that the multiculturalism programme of the Department of Canadian Heritage as a publicly funded programme should end, in many ways this has already occurred. The Progressive Conservative Party, at its recent policy convention in Winnipeg, maintained as a guiding principle that Canada as a multicultural society is a sociological fact. Indeed, the PC delegates insisted that a PC government would, as a policy priority, value this reality and accept the duty to foster understanding and equality of opportunity while promoting the common values that Canadians share.[4]

FUTURE OUTLOOK

Public policy in Canada for the year 2000 must give expression to the reality of multiculturalism as a fundamental characteristic of Canadian society. It must also give programmatic expression to promoting race relations and equality of opportunity. All of these dimensions are critical elements of Canadian citizenship and the values we share. The fact that Canadians can trace their origins and their arduous destinies to the four corners of the globe speaks to the richness of Canada's heritage. Canada's identity is inclusive of the many cultures which reflect who we are as a society, where we have come from, and affords the country great opportunity in the bluebell society of the next century.

Multiculturalism is a dynamic of Canada's citizenry and unity. An active Canadian citizenship is the responsibility of all Canadians. In addition, clearer understanding of the "community of communities", perhaps through the enhancement of Canadian Studies programmes, will further a society that is open and inclusive of all ethnocultural communities.

CONCLUSION

History defines the present; it is not something to set aside in pursuit of a better tomorrow. Canadian governments must continue to be respectful of the varied histories of the nation's people so together we can grow stronger and more secure in the knowledge that the grand Canadian experiment will survive and even thrive.

Hugh MacLennan in his *Two Solitudes* quoted a line of poetry, "...that two solitudes meet, greet and protect each other." I think it appropriate for Canadians and their government to expand MacLennan's use of the prose to the "us" and "them" solitudes that are sometimes part of the Canadian reality. Multiculturalism and unity go hand-in-hand. We must work to support the growth and development of the shared values necessary for the creation of a vibrant and active citizenship.

(In the Summer of 1996 the Progressive Conservative Party convention voted to abolish the federal multiculturalism policy.)

NOTES

1 Morton, William L. "A Note on the Second Edition" in *The Canadian Identity,* 2nd ed. Toronto: University of Toronto Press, 1972, p. VI. Professor Morton once wrote: "...the brute fact in Canadian history is distance."

2 Castrilli, Anna Marie P. (National President, National Congress of Italian Canadians). "Written Brief on *Bill C-18, An Act to Establish the Department of Multiculturalism and Citizenship,* to Senator Lorna Marsden, Chair of the Senate Standing Committee on Social Affairs, Science and Technology", October 29, 1990, p. 12.

3 See: "'Canadian Citizenship: Sharing the responsibility', The Seventeenth Report of the Standing Senate Committee on Social Affairs, Science and Technology", May 1993, p. 28.

4 "A Multicultural Society" in *Report of the Policy Advisory Committee: Designing a Blueprint for Canadians*, July 1996, pp. 80-83.

INDEPENDENT MP: CULTURE AS AN INDIVIDUAL RESPONSIBILILTY

Jan Brown

The following is an edited speech given by Jan Brown in the House of Commons on April 5, 1995. At the time, Mrs. Brown was a Reform Party Member of Parliament for Calgary Southeast. She left the Reform Party in May 1996 to sit as an Independent, and has since become a member of the Progressive Conservative Party.

Motion:

> *That in the opinion of this house, the government should transfer the responsibility for cultural preservation to individuals by discontinuing federal multiculturalism programs, relinquishing control of multiculturalism thereby allowing multiculturalism to flourish by giving individuals the freedom to pursue their own cultural ideals.*

Mr. Speaker, I am pleased to move this motion this evening. Canadians from all across this country have become involved in a debate that explores the merits of the federal government's policy on multiculturalism. The issue has its defenders and its detractors. But most significantly, people no longer are blindly accepting the status quo that multiculturalism funding should be beyond reproach or even be beyond questioning.

The position of the Reform Party is given expression in my motion as just read. By relinquishing control at the federal level for funding multicultural projects, we will also be giving to individuals the chance to choose for themselves what cultural endeavours they wish to support.

As a government we have diminishing resources and as individual taxpayers we too have less and less disposable income. It is in light of this that we as legislators should be making efforts to maximize the freedom of individuals to distribute their disposable income where they choose.

In contemporary Canada does it not seem a little arrogant when the government decides which programs, which groups and which individuals should be funded? Are these decisions not better left in the hands of Canadians and not government? Why is it that this Liberal government avoids all of the difficult decisions that concern Canadians the most?

Let me share with the House some sentiments from an average Canadian. I recently spoke to a group in Kingston, Ontario about my vision for Canada. A woman who heard me that day sent me some of her thoughts, which echo mine. I would like to share them with the House today. She wrote on something she called "Acceptable Behaviour in a Global Village". She wrote:

> *The world of human beings has grown smaller and populations all over the world have become so mixed that we have to learn to get along peacefully with each other. The global village is no longer somewhere else. It is here and all of us are mixed in with it. It does not matter whether someone of a different race or nation lives next door or down the street or in a different part of town or halfway around the world, we have to learn to live peacefully with all of those peoples whose racial or national origins are different from our own. To do otherwise is to bring about an end to our world. The intolerance, conflicts, fighting and wars between peoples will bring*

an end to our civilization and the earth as a planet much quicker than any pollution or natural disaster.

All peoples have some members who are great people, who have accomplished things which are beneficial for all humankind. All peoples have some members who are difficult people who make life miserable for those around them. No one is perfect. Most people of all races are a mixture of good and bad. It is necessary to recognize the best and the positive in others regardless of what they look like, what language they speak, or where they come from. The positive values of honesty, integrity, the ability to do the job required of them, the ability to care for family and other people, and the ability to live peacefully together with others— all provide the basis for a good and worthwhile society.

Every race and nation of people has those individuals whose performance is excellent in all of those values. Every race and nation has many who fail to uphold those positive values. We need to change our attitudes to become more objective and non-judgmental. We need to become more accepting of all people.

The woman concludes her letter with the thought that:

This is not an easy thing to do but if enough of us who feel this necessity start to put these attitudes into our own lives and encourage others to also do so, we will have a better world.

These are the sentiments of an ordinary Canadian. The writer has no Ph.D. in peace issues. She has no certificates proclaiming her to be an expert on eliminating racial discrimination. But she clearly is an expert on old-fashioned Canadian common sense. If we could only bottle these common sense attitudes and ship them throughout Canada and around the world, what a better place this would be.

I was mentioning earlier that the issue of multiculturalism is of high profile in the media of late. I was reading a recent edition of *India Abroad* in which Professor Milton Israel wrote about the issue of identity as it pertains to multiculturalism. He wrote:

> *For some the emphasis on ethnicity facilitates division; for others, it provides a means to cope and a possibility of unity on better terms. Still others insist that national boundaries and the limited and distinctive identities they produce are eroding and the future lies with the "transnationals", people who are at home m more than one society. The loss of old home through migration or the substantial immigration of others is not to be lamented, but a new kind of cosmopolitan nationalism is to be embraced.*

I share this view. We do not need a special dispensation from the government to foster this belief. Members of ethnic communities also espouse these views. I experienced this when I spoke to the Human Rights and Race Relations Centre in Toronto, a privately funded organization that works to end discrimination in Canada. I went there on March 21 which was a day that acknowledged a race-free society. In fact it was called "the day to eliminate racism in the world".

I was so impressed that day with the individuals I met. They were all volunteers, leaders from the ethnic communities in Toronto. They had strived, free of federal government funding, to bring together other community leaders to discuss the issue of racial discrimination in the hope that it could be eliminated in this century.

There was a wonderful letter in the conference package that had been written by the Honourable Paul Martin Jr. He said he wished to acknowledge the work and contribution of the Human Rights and Race Relations Centre toward ending racial discrimination in this country. He acknowledged the dedication and commitment demonstrated by the staff and the volunteers—indeed all of them in this centre are volunteers—

and that their efforts had been exemplary. He said that they all deserved to be commended for their efforts.

This is an excellent example of a group of Canadians who are working together without government funding to support and to further the process to eliminate discrimination.

The Reform Party opposes the current concept of multiculturalism and hyphenated Canadianism pursued by the Government of Canada. We would end funding of the multiculturalism program and support the abolition of the department and the Secretary of State for Multiculturalism.

If the Minister of Finance sincerely wants ideas on how to cut the deficit he will get rid of this aspect of special interest funding. He would immediately save the taxpayers of Canada some $38.8 million a year. This also sends a powerful message to all concerned that beliefs in self-reliance, the indomitable spirit of the self in search of autonomy and independence is encouraged and championed in Canada.

Multiculturalism was introduced in the House of Commons on October 8, 1971. In the 23 years that have followed, it has been politically incorrect for anyone to criticize it. I will repeat that. It has been politically incorrect for anyone to criticize it, especially in the House of Commons. I do not know the number of times I have had to bear the label of being bigoted because I speak from a different point of view. I have no patience for that any longer when all I want to do is bring reasoned and rational debate to this issue.

In fact, members of Parliament from the Tories, the Grits and the NDP have all used the multiculturalism policy in a way that I believe is insincere, superficial and shallow in order to garner political support from ethnic communities.

We all want the right to retain our roots, but what we have is Trudeau's enforced multicultural scam and the costs have been excessive. Ethnic group is pitted against ethnic group and the country is fragmented into a thousand consciousnesses. Trudeau's ideas about multiculturalism continue to contribute as a primary factor in the erosion of federalism and Canada's unity. Catering to special interest groups *à la* Trudeau and company smashes the spine of federalism. This destructive outcome is almost inevitable so long as we officially encourage large groups to remain apart from the mainstream.

The multiculturalism policy of Canada was designed to "recognize and promote the understanding that multiculturalism reflects the cultural and racial diversity of Canadian society and acknowledges the freedom of all members of Canadian society to preserve, enhance and share their cultural heritage". It is intended to "promote full and equitable participation of individuals and communities of all origins" in all aspects of Canadian life, including "equal treatment and equal protection under the law, while respecting and valuing their diversity". The language of the policy is fairly innocuous and well meaning, but in practice it endorses special interest groups' agendas at the expense of the taxpayer.

Canadians remain unsure of what multiculturalism is, what it is trying to do and why and what it can accomplish in a free and democratic society such as ours. Multiculturalism can encompass folk songs, dance, food, festivals, arts and crafts, museums, heritage languages, ethnic studies, ethnic presses, race relations, culture sharing and human rights. Much of the opposition to multiculturalism results from the indiscriminate application of the term to a wide range of situations, practices, expectations and goals as well as its institutionalization as state policy—an expensive one at that.

Public support for multiculturalism has been difficult to ascertain. In the early 1970s when the Royal Commission on Bilingualism and Biculturalism recommended the government introduce some ethnocultural policy, public support for multiculturalism was at around 76 per cent.

An Angus Reid poll in 1991 showed that figure has not changed much. It remains at 78 per cent. But what can we make of this level of support? Little to nothing, I suggest. At the same time that poll was being done, the Citizens' Forum on Canada's Future reported some uneasiness about the Canadian public's attitude toward multiculturalism policies. It stated:

> *Overwhelmingly, participants told us that reminding us of our different origins is less useful in binding a unified country than emphasizing the things we have in common. While Canadians accept and value Canada's cultural diversity, they do not value many of the activities of the multicultural program of the federal government. These are seen as expensive and divisive in that they remind Canadians of their different origins rather than their shared symbols, society and future.*

Further to this, a Decima survey was commissioned by the Canadian Council of Christians and Jews and was carried out in October 1993. The survey found that three out of four Canadians expressed a preference for an American style melting pot approach to immigration over the multicultural mosaic that has been officially promoted in Canada since the 1970s.

The survey also disclosed that Canadians generally are increasingly intolerant of interest group demands and that there is a relatively strong view that, in particular, ethnic, racial or religious minorities must make more efforts to adapt to Canada rather than insisting upon a maintenance of difference, especially at federal expense. Roughly similar proportions of visible minorities expressed the same sentiments.

This poll would suggest that it is the prevalent opinion amongst the groups targeted to receive multiculturalism grants that such grants are divisive. These are not my words; they come from others.

As I mentioned, criticism of the status quo has been increasing from the policy's supposed beneficiaries. For example, a fellow by the name of Jimmy who emigrated from Vietnam in 1980 and is now a technician at a photo processing lab commented: "The government spends too much money on something that's not necessary. Canada has freedom and work for anyone who wants it, and that is all newcomers need." In Richmond, a magazine editor by the name of Anthony agreed that government-sanctioned segregation is no good for Canada.

What seems to be clear is that there is an erosion of support for multiculturalism by the citizens of Canada. This erosion of support for the multicultural approach, particularly given that minorities themselves concur, does nothing to promote harmony and unity in Canada because it does not recognize that all Canadians are equal.

Our vision of Canada should be committed to the goal of social and personal well-being that values individuality while emphasizing themes like family and community assumption of responsibility, problem-solving and communicating these value-sets as a means to better group life. However, at no time should the rights of a group supersede the rights of individuals, unless the group happens to consist of a majority within Canada.

I have tried to show why the federal government's interpretations of multicultural support must come to an end. We can no longer spend money we do not have on financing such a notion. The Angus Reid study from 1991 clearly shows that not only has the multicultural program failed, but Canadians oppose it. One of the main reasons that Canadians oppose this policy is because it is divisive.

I would like to refer to Arthur Slessinger, Jr. Mr. Slessinger is not a conservative thinker whom I trot out to support my position. He is a well-known liberal, an American Democrat. He is the quintessential Liberal's liberal. Slessinger believes that, by its very nature, multiculturalism is dangerously divisive. It encourages government to segregate citizens along racial, ethnic and linguistic fault-lines. Then it compels them to dole out rights and money according to the labels people wear. Far better to focus on unifying forces, he advises, emphasizing the characteristics, desires and beliefs that citizens hold in common. Otherwise, tribal hostilities will drive them apart.

Preservation of diverse cultural heritages can be left to individuals, families and private self-financing organizations.

In closing, I would like to acknowledge that my own personal circumstances are those that encompass a multicultural family. I have a daughter who has dual citizenship with Australia and Canada. I have another daughter who is married to a young man from Mexico; his name is Fernando Rodriguez. I have European roots myself, Croatian and Norwegian. My husband also has a European background. Our family is multicultural. It reflects very much the diversity and richness of those various cultures.

I speak as a Reformer in this House. I believe there is no place in our society for the federal government to continue to fund multiculturalism. However, I do believe that there is a price to be paid for forging a new nationality of diverse elements. Simply put, there is a fair degree of tolerance and goodwill all around. I have learned that through my personal experience.

RACE, EQUALITY AND JUSTICE IN CANADA

MULTICULTURALISM, JEWS, AND THE FORGING OF A CANADIAN IDENTITY

Irving Abella

Being a Jew in Canada today means being able to celebrate and participate freely in all of this country's wonderful possibilities. Canada today is a generous country, far different from the benighted, xenophobic, anti-semitic country it once was. Only a generation or two ago Jews were excluded from almost every sector of Canadian society and some were even excluded from the country itself by a government and a people who felt there were already too many Jews here.

This is an enormous country with a tiny Jewish population. Though the Canadian Jewish community is now the fourth largest in the Diaspora and growing quickly, we ought not to get too haughty. Remember there are more Jews in Chicago and almost as many in greater Philadelphia than in all of Canada. And as for all Canadians, life for Jews is influenced by the vastness of the land. If Jews suffer from an excess of history, Canadians suffer from an excess of geography—Canadian Jews suffer from both. We are the world's largest small nation. That sense of smallness and the immensity of the country may well have contributed to a sense of insecurity and marginality that has dominated the Canadian Jewish community for too much of this century.

Some joker once said that you can tell a Canadian by the fact that when he or she walks into a room, he or she automatically chooses to sit on the most uncomfortable chair. It is part of our apparent genetic affinity for discomfort and self-denial that has formed the Canadian character as clearly as has our geography. If Americans are the world's missionaries, intent on changing it, we Canadians are respectful members of the congregation. And we like it. We are, it seems, a country full of solutions looking for problems.

And if there is anything we are noted for, aside from our hockey players and, dare I say it—modesty—it is that we are pioneers in the creation of a multicultural society. Multiculturalism is protected by our laws; it is entrenched in our new Charter of Rights; and it is defended and, more important, funded by a special cabinet-level government department. Multiculturalism is a wonderful policy. And I say that as a Canadian and as a Jew and, of course, as President of the Canadian Jewish Congress. Multiculturalism is innovative; it has enhanced our self-image; it has proven a life-saver to many communities; it has created pride where there had once only been pain; comfort where there was once only contempt; and it has given Canadians a sense of uniqueness.

Multiculturalism emerged in Canada in the 1960s from a quest for identity and acceptance by upwardly mobile second and third-generation European immigrants. It developed in reaction to French-Canadian nationalism and as a response to a government effort to define Canada as bicultural. Ethnic communities asked the unanswerable questions: if it is valuable for French Canadians to maintain their distinctive culture and identity, why is it not so for other groups?[1]

The fact is that unlike the United States, we in Canada were never concerned only with the rights of individuals. Our historical roots involved as well a constitutional appreciation of two groups, French and English, as distinct and unassimilated and yet theoretically of equal worth and entitlement. That is, unlike the United States, whose individualism promoted assimilation, we in Canada have always conceded that the right to integrate based on differences has as much legal and political integrity as the right to assimilate. A melting pot, if necessary, but not necessarily a melting pot.

So, on the one hand, we find different groups trying to integrate their distinctiveness into the mainstream and on the other hand we find other groups trying to keep them or their distinctiveness out by setting homogenizing terms and conditions at the gate.

What makes us unique is our pluralist culture. The Canadian mosaic is our national cliché; it is our single most important national characteristic. Here, all of us—the country's founding peoples of British and French origin, plus other Europeans, Asians, Africans, West Indians, Latin Americans, Catholics, Muslims, Hindus, Sikhs, and Jews—arrived trailing our own roots, which are now firmly transplanted into fertile new ground. And along with Canada's First Nations, we have built a new country. What makes Canada so special is the unwritten compact that bigotry will not be condoned, that instead of abusing one another, we can always talk out our problems and sometimes even our prejudices.

We are unique as well because not only do we have freedom of speech, we have freedom from speech. We do not allow hatemongers to peddle their poison publicly. We protect our minorities because we respect both their contributions and their sensitivities.

And yet, sadly, those values we once gloried in as a nation are under attack. It is clear that racism is on the rise throughout the industrial world. We see it everywhere; we hear it on the ubiquitous "talk radio" shows; we watch it on television; we feel it. We don't need public opinion polls to corroborate it, but they do. Intolerance, it seems, is the growth industry of the 1990s.

Canada is a peculiar nation. It is a country of immigrants that hates immigration. Almost every public opinion poll done over the past fifty years indicates that most Canadians, including apparently immigrants themselves, do not want any substantial increase in the number of people admitted into the country. Given their image of themselves, this attitude may surprise many Canadians; historically, however, it should not.

Most Canadians take pride in their history, their traditions, their heritage, and especially their myths. And if there is a pervasive Canadian myth—something most Canadians grew up with, were taught in their schools, or were accustomed to hearing from their politicians—it is that our country is one of immigrants, one with a long history of welcoming refugees and dissidents.

Racism and bigotry, most Canadians were raised to believe, are European—or at least American—inventions that have little part in Canadian history or even the country's psyche. Canada, it has been constantly hammered home to its citizenry, is a country of wide open space and immeasurable wealth, a country that has always been open and available to those proverbial "huddled masses yearning to be free".

This attitude was best summarized by a witness testifying in Ottawa before the Senate Committee on Immigration in 1946: "To our ancestors," he said, "the flag which floated over them was a symbol of the rights of sanctuary which it offered to the victims of tyranny and inequality in every other part of the world." He added: "They ... never questioned the obligation to admit those who were fleeing from oppression elsewhere."[2]

Yet few took notice of the churlish response of some of the senators. Surely this "right of sanctuary", they asked, did not include Orientals and Negroes? There was no response. None was necessary; everyone knew the answer.

For most of our history, Canada's immigration policy has been racist and exclusionary. We knew exactly what kind of people we wanted and how to keep out those we did not. Our immigration acts were so designed as to divide the world in two: the preferred races, who were always welcome in Canada, and the non-preferred, who rarely were.

Specifically written into the legislation were those races and peoples in descending order of preference who could be allowed into the country. At the top were British and white Americans, who were always acceptable. When economic necessity dictated the admission of non-British, non-American stock, immigration officials were given a list of desirable peoples. Following the British and American were northern Europeans, then central Europeans, and finally southern and eastern Europeans. At the bottom of the list were Jews, followed by Asians and Blacks.

Occasionally, during periods of economic boom, these non-preferred immigrants were acceptable so long as they remained out of sight, risking life and limb in the mines and smelters of the west, holed up in the lumber camps deep in the forest, or packed into stuffy, unventilated sweatshops in urban centres.

The central problem of Canadian immigration policy for most of our history is that we never had one. In the 128 years that we have existed as a nation, we have had exactly four immigration acts. There never has been in Canada, either now or in the past, any clearly articulated national consensus about what immigration should be or should do. Except for one constant—its discriminatory aspect—our policies have had little consistency. Until recently, Canadian governments have rarely felt obliged to proclaim clearly defined, long-range immigration objectives, whether demographic, economic, or social. As one critic remarked: "Canadian immigration thinking has been an exercise in sustaining an uneasy balance among a variety of forces all tugging in different directions."[3] As a result, it has been an issue which over the years has divided Canadians far more than it has united them.

Thus, it was not until the 1950s, fully 85 years after we became a nation and after the country had accepted millions of immigrants, that it was felt necessary to create a permanent, free-standing Department of Immigration, with its own minister. Until then, immigration was apparently so little thought of that its responsibilities were often passed back and forth among reluctant departments—clearly an indication of how little respect, or thought, was given to immigration policy. At one time or another, immigration matters were lumped together with such departments as Agriculture, Interior, and even Indian Affairs and Mines and Natural Resources.

Thus immigration and refugee policy has until recent times largely been in the hands of a small group of bureaucrats. Throughout most of our history, and certainly until the 1950s, it was this tiny group that by default orchestrated our immigration policy. Their historical role - and most of them saw it this way as well—was not so much to find ways to encourage people to come to Canada as to find ways to keep them out. They were gatekeepers concerned only to open the gates when economic pressures forced them to, and then only as narrowly as they could.

Their efforts were naturally applauded by successive Canadian governments. Immigration officials were simply doing their job and, in the eyes of most Canadians, doing it well. They were clearly reflecting the nativist, xenophobic attitudes that permeated the Canada of an earlier period.

Indeed, it was not until the 1960s that Canada finally abandoned its racially discriminatory policies and opened itself to immigrants from places that had never before been recognized as potential sources for new Canadians: the Caribbean, Latin America, the Middle East, and Asia. And ironically, given our history, the majority of new immigrants and refugees now arriving in Canada are from these areas.

For many Canadians, as the polls show, that is a real problem. Unpalatable as it is, we must confront reality. There are significant numbers of Canadians, the opinion surveys indicate, who do not like what is happening to their country. To many, Canada is beginning to look like the United Nations, and they do not like it at all. There are too many brown, yellow, and black faces on their city streets and subways for their liking.

And the anecdotal evidence about anti-immigrant feeling is supported by recent opinion polls that indicate growing hostility and opposition to both immigration and, for the first time, what used to be a unifying factor in this country: multiculturalism. These polls reveal that large numbers of Canadians feel that minority groups are too "pushy", that they are demanding too many rights, that they are too "noisy", and that they try to be "where they are not wanted".[4]

Perhaps the most revealing aspect of these surveys is that a significant number of Canadians believe that immigrants and visible minorities—the public no longer seems to differentiate between the two—should be restricted in terms of how much influence they are permitted to exercise over the future of this country. Many Canadians report that they get very angry when they see new immigrants on television demanding the same rights as other Canadians. They believe that immigrants are themselves responsible for the growing intolerance in this country.

Above all, many see multiculturalism as a divisive force in Canada, as a waste of public money, and as a surefire guarantee that Canadians will never develop their own identity. They feel that the changing face of Canadian society is changing too quickly and in directions they do not appreciate. This face, they believe, will soon be totally unrecognizable and unfamiliar.

The burning, all-encompassing issue for Canadians today is how this country will survive as a nation. What must be done to keep us together and united into the next century and beyond? And one of the basic questions is whether multiculturalism helps or hinders this drive for national unity. Does it divide more than it unites us? As we grope to find or create a common cultural and national spirit, does multiculturalism advance or hinder us in our pursuit?

What is happening to the almost mythical Canadian mosaic? Is it becoming a melting pot, or, even worse, a pressure cooker? What is the future of multiculturalism in Canada? Are we the model other countries should strive to emulate or, as many are now suggesting, the model of what to avoid?

From my perspective as a historian, the origins of a multicultural policy are quite simple to explain. Aside from addressing the usual political considerations, multiculturalism came into being in order to open minds that for too long had been closed. It aimed to make new Canadians feel more welcome in their chosen new home and to remind Canadians of older standing of their heritage and cultural background. Above all, it was to remind all Canadians that this is not simply a nation of two founding peoples, that other groups, especially Aboriginal peoples and millions of immigrants, have played an important but often ignored role in this country's growth and development. The original purpose of multiculturalism was to right a terrible historical wrong and to write these peoples back into Canadian history.

Many Canadians believe that multiculturalism in Canada is an admission of failure. For two generations, from the beginning of mass immigration at the turn of the century through the 1950s, Canadian authorities, teachers, clerics, politicians, and journalists—the people who set a tone for society—sought desperately to assimilate new immigrants, to persuade them to forsake their strange languages, their alien customs, their exotic religions, and to assimilate. They failed, and for an obvious reason. Unlike in the United States, there was nothing for the immigrants to assimilate into. There was no Canadian nationality, no discernible culture, no unique identity, no myths, no ethos, no overweening national heroes. We were missing everything Americans had. We had no Hollywood to manufacture heroes, we had no glorious revolution to overthrow an evil tyrant, no bloody civil war to free the slaves; we had no Statue of Liberty, no Washingtons, no Jeffersons or Lincolns.

The United States was born with the stirring Declaration of Independence and its rhapsodic exhortation to Americans to commit themselves to the inspiring pursuit of life, liberty, and happiness. Our country was born with the rather less stirring, very prosaic 72 resolutions of the Quebec Conference and the British North America Act, with their somewhat less than triumphant, very pedestrian challenge to Canadians to set their goal as a nation to achieve peace, order, and good government. We Canadians have no pledge of allegiance—to whom would we pledge allegiance? Indeed, we did not even have our own flag until 30 years ago. We have a constitution that was created originally by another country's parliament and that we could not even amend until 15 years ago; and we only recently got an official national anthem, of which, according to a recent survey, the majority of adult Canadians don't even know the words.

Several years ago, a survey of English Canadian teenagers revealed the following about their heros.[5] Their favourite politician was George Bush; their favourite athlete was Michael Jordan; their favourite television program was Beverly Hills 90210; their favourite news broadcaster was Dan Rather; and their favourite author—and this, in the land of Margaret Atwood, Robertson Davies, and Leonard Cohen—was Stephen King. Not a Canadian among them.

Well, of course there is a strong nationalism in Canada and has been for 300 years. But it is the sentiment of some 7 million people who live in Quebec and who speak French as their mother tongue. The nationalism of the French Canadian is the sentiment of a relatively small, homogeneous, religiously, culturally, and historically-conscious community that uses its nationalism in the name of self-preservation.

But the fact that there is no single Canadian people or culture makes it easier for minority groups such as Jews to maintain a separate identity and even a separate culture, to grow and to flourish. Where everyone is a hyphenated Canadian, Jews do not stand out from others when they include their Jewish as well as their Canadian element in their identity. Because the bulk of our community consists of immigrants who came during this century or their descendants, the encouragement of ethnic distinctiveness is very important in creating an environment in which Jews can live comfortably as Jews while participating in all aspects of Canadian society.

Not surprisingly, in Canada there has evolved a Jewish community that is more traditional, more unified, closer to the old country, and more culturally homogeneous than that in the United States. While American Jews were joyfully entering into the mainstream of the great republic, Canadian Jews could easily maintain their Jewishness in a country that had no coherent self-definition and whose mainstream was for so long closed to Jews. Responding to their environment, Canadian Jews created institutions and organizations that allow them to build a community and maintain it within a multicultural and increasingly secular society.[6]

For example, the Canadian Jewish Congress is a unique organization, with no American counterpart. In the United States, there is no single organization that can reasonably claim to represent the entire Jewish community, as the Congress can in Canada. It is precisely because for so many years Canadian Jewry had felt far more threatened than American Jewry that the Congress came into being. It was created to fight the virulent anti-Semitism that permeated Canada in the interwar years.

Most of our country's Jewish institutions emerged directly out of the vitality of eastern European Jewry, in the years between 1880 and 1930. Thus the Jews who founded the Canadian Jewish community were more "Jewish" in the cultural, national, and religious sense than those who founded the American Jewish community. This, I think, has had profound consequences, slowing assimilation within Canadian Jewry and creating an institutional fabric that is more traditional and separatist than its counterpart. Thus, Jews in Canada still remain a distinct group, caught between two of Canada's founding communities and yet capitalizing on the shift from bi- to multiculturalism.[7]

Let us not forget another factor. American Jewry, at least until 1900, was dominated by German immigrants who had arrived in the nineteenth century. Their wealth and influence allowed Jews to merge into the American mainstream long before Canadian Jews forced themselves into the Canadian mainstream. Their patriotism was more to their American than to their Jewish identity. That is probably why Zionism took hold much sooner and much stronger in Canada than in the United States. In Canada, the issue of double loyalty never arose among Jews the way it did south of the border because historically there was no demand here to overtly display loyalty to the nation state. It would have been unthinkable, indeed impossible, as historian Gerald Tulchinsky has observed, for a Canadian Jew to write a counterpart to Irving Berlin's jingoist *God Bless America.*[8] There would be no *God Bless Canada.* We did not share that chauvinism. No Canadian Jew could have written a panegyric to a Canadian river the way an American Jew, Jerome Kern, exalted and rhapsodized the old Mississippi. We did not share that attachment to our history. Our great rivers—the Mackenzie, the St. Lawrence, the Fraser—have little resonance to Canadian Jewry. Nor could a Canadian Jew have glorified a state the way Richard Rodgers and Oscar Hammerstein II immortalized Oklahoma. It boggles the mind to imagine a Miriam Waddington, an A.M. Klein, or even a Mordechai Richler canonizing Saskatchewan.

All the indicators reveal that Canadian Jews identify themselves more strongly as Jews than do their American counterparts. They have lower rates of intermarriage, go to Israel more often, donate more money to Jewish causes, are more Zionistic, more Orthodox, more likely to know or speak Hebrew or Yiddish, have as their closest friends other Jews, and are more likely to send their children to Jewish day schools.[9]

In America, Jews are defined, often even by themselves, as a religious group. Here, Jews are more likely to be identified as an ethnic group. American Jews are more widely integrated into American politics and culture: whereas there are now over fifty Jews in the

American Congress, there are only three in the Canadian House of Commons.

The American Jewish experience is a different one—not a better one. We Canadian Jews have a history every bit as illustrious, which we ought to be proud of, if only we knew it. It is time to put to rest the canard that Canadian Jews are in a time lag, that we are a generation behind American Jews. Yes, we are a generation closer to Europe, but our history in Canada is as old and as interesting as Jewish history in the United States.

There is one significant fact about the history of Canadian Jewry that needs reiteration because so few of us, and so few other Canadians—including our historians—know it. There has been a Jewish presence in this country almost from the beginning of European settlement. We are not newcomers. Jews preceded almost every immigrant group, including perhaps the English.[10] There has been a constant, uninterrupted Jewish presence in Canada for at least 250 years. It was a French Jew from Bordeaux who helped finance, feed, supply, and generally keep afloat early French settlement in Canada in the eighteenth century. When the British landed in Louisbourg, Nova Scotia, to plant the Union Jack, they were preceded by a small number of Portuguese Jews. When General Wolfe launched his attack on Quebec, which captured Canada for the British, one of the ships in his flotilla was commanded by an officer of Jewish descent.

It would probably surprise most Canadians to learn that in the 1770s and 1780s the fur trade was dominated by a consortium of Jewish merchants. As the most important traders of the period, they helped establish the European presence in large parts of Canada previously unplotted by the newcomers. They built and supplied a network of trading posts, and negotiated with the Indians, some almost losing their lives when dealings turned hostile.

More importantly, there were Jewish office-holders in Canada long before Jews were permitted to hold government positions in Britain or anywhere else in the British Empire. And years before Jews were allowed to hold seats in the British Parliament, Jews were elected to the legislatures in Canada. It was the tiny Jewish community in this country that some 150 years ago led the battle to adopt the first Charter of Political Rights in the British Empire and whose victory forced the British to change their attitude toward Jews in Britain.

Thus the Jewish contribution to this country began long before most people suspect and was profoundly important right from the start.

At the beginning of this century, the world of Canadian Jewry was the world of the Jewish farmer, small-town storekeeper, and factory worker. You could get on the CPR transcontinental in Halifax and travel across the country to Vancouver, and in almost every town, village, or hamlet in eastern or western Canada through which the train passed there was a Jewish family or two. There were stations along the CPR main line named after a Mr. Levine, a Mr. Katz, and a Mr. Oungre, who was head of the Hebrew Immigrant Aid Society in Europe. There were towns and villages with Jewish names such as Hirsch and Lipton, and there were even three public school districts in Saskatchewan named the Herzl, Yeshurun, and Tifereth Yisroel, though non-Jewish students referred to the latter as "Typhus Israel".

The Jewish farmer and small-town storekeeper were largely a one generation phenomenon in Canada, as was the Jewish factory worker. Despite the enormous contribution to Canadian society of the Jewish labour movement, a contribution we are only now beginning to appreciate, it lasted for little more than one generation. Workers scrimped, saved, and sacrificed to make certain that their children would never work in a factory. And they succeeded, thus dooming the Jewish trade union movement.

For Jews, these decades were a period of dreadful living and working conditions, of poverty, want, and hardship; yet they also created a Jewish world full of vitality, spirit, experimentation, passion, and creativity. The Jews of the time were tearing off the fetters of the Old World and accommodating to the exigencies of the New. The community of a generation or two ago was in constant ideological turmoil, as the religious fought a rearguard action against the new secularists; as Zionists argued with Bundists, and Socialists clashed with Communists; as territorialists, culturalists, revisionists, separatists, and integrationists all had a go at one another. All had conflicting agendas for their survival as Jews; together, they made the Jewish pot boil.

It was an era of revered institutions that have also passed from the Jewish scene. It was the world of the urban Yiddish press, of the Adler, the Djurnal, the Yiddishe Wort, of the Yiddish theatre, with dozens of home-grown acting troupes, as well as regular visits from the fabled Yiddish actors and actresses of New York or Warsaw. It was the world of the wonderfully unique Jewish bookstores such as Hyman's and Harshman's, which were more meeting halls than bookstores, where newcomers, old-timers, students, workers, radicals, and manufacturers would gather to browse through the books but mostly to meet friends, drink seltzer water, and argue their views late into the night.

Lamentably, these have all disappeared. And so, to a large extent, have most of the great communal organizations of the time. The Arbeiter Ring, the Farband, and the Landsmenschaften still linger on, but their dynamism is spent. Gone too are the Labour Lyceum, Coronation Hall, and the Monument National Theatre. And though they still exist, the Main, Spadina, and Selkirk Avenues are no longer part of the Jewish world. They have slipped into our mythical past and have become part of our historical memory, though etched forever into the Canadian Jewish psyche.

Simply to romanticize our past and bask in nostalgia would be wrong. This was also a period of government quotas, restrictions, and boycotts. The Canada of the first 50 years of this century was permeated with racism, xenophobia, and anti-Semitism. Jews were at the bottom of Canadian society—despised, demeaned, and discriminated against.

There is a commonly held belief among Canadians today that the Jewish community is politically and economically powerful and always has been. Yet just over a generation ago, the Jew was the pariah of Canadian society, the target of abuse, excluded from most professions and legally prevented from living and vacationing in a wide variety of areas from coast to coast.

Few opportunities were available to Jews: Most firms did not hire Jews; Jews were largely barred from the civil services; most hospitals were closed to Jewish doctors—and when one was finally given a job as an intern in Montreal, his fellow interns went out on strike until he was fired. Universities publicly restricted Jewish student enrolment; shockingly, there was not one Jewish professor in any Canadian university in the period, in a world awash with renowned Jewish refugee scientists and academics from Germany desperately seeking jobs. Indeed, as we now know, the very country closed itself to Jews. In perhaps the most shameful act in its history, Canada turned its back and locked its gates to the doomed Jews of Europe frantically seeking to escape the Nazi scourge. In so doing, Canada had the worst record of any Western country in providing sanctuary to Jewish refugees.

Ironically, the country's most telling and symbolic export in these years was the thousands of talented, motivated young Jewish men and women who, closed off from contributing to their society, emigrated south to make their mark in the United States.

For Canadian Jewry, a new period of its development was ushered in after the Second World War. The raucous dynamism that marked the earlier phase of Jewish life was abruptly stilled by the trauma of the Holocaust and by the fragility of the tiny new Jewish state in the Middle East. The world had become too dangerous a place for Jews to allow themselves the luxury of internal dissent and divisiveness. The old economic tensions within the community dissipated. The radicalism and feistiness of the 1920s and 1930s seemed sadly out of place in the changed world of the 1960s and 1970s.

In any case, Jewish energies were now totally devoted to protecting the state of Israel, to welcoming the influx of Holocaust survivors, and to breaking down barriers in Canadian society. It was the "*sha shtil*" generation, afraid to rock the boat for fear of sinking with it. And so Jews hunkered down to their work while at the same time charging full-steam ahead into a rapidly opening-up Canadian society. With the help of suddenly sympathetic politicians, government, and courts, Jewish community leaders, trade unionists, and lawyers successfully lobbied for anti-discrimination, fair-employment, and housing legislation. With astonishing rapidity, we tore down these barriers, thus opening up Canadian society not only for us but for other immigrant and ethnic minority groups.

The past twenty years have been revolutionary for Canadian Jewry. Doors long closed have been pushed wide open. Who would have thought a generation ago that the Canada of the 1970s and 1980s would have Jewish premiers, cabinet ministers, chief justices, ambassadors, and university presidents? Nothing, it seems, is barred to us today. The barriers are all down, except for the psychological ones.

Let us face facts. Despite our successes, despite our achievements, despite our status in Canada, there is a general sense of disquiet, of unease and frustration in the community. As a Jewish Yogi Berra might have put it: "If everything is so good, then why is everything so bad?" Rhetoric aside, the question strikes straight into the heart of the Jewish dilemma. The strange balance between hope and despair, between good news and bad news, is, of course, common in the Jewish condition.

According to every survey, Canadian Jews are the most comfortable, integrated, and educated communities in the country. We have social, financial, and even political clout, which we have never had before. There is no area in Canadian society in which we do not play an important role. We are the envy of every Jewish community in the world, and if we were not, we should be.

Canadian Jews live in a society in which Jewish lives are not in danger. What is in danger is Jewish life—and to many that is equally serious. Growing assimilation and intermarriage rates in the United States are a real concern to Canadian Jews. In North America, living as a Jew is only one option among many. No external force imposes it on us or forces us to live in ghettos or wear badges or carry identifying labels in our passports. And when living as a Jew is a choice, we must be able to offer our children more than simply an invitation to survive. We must provide something better and more saleable than the other options. When the brightest of our young ask us what it is that our survival will make possible, we should have answers for them—if we have any. What are we Jews about? What dream do we fulfill by surviving?

It seems to me self-evident what the major challenge to our Jewish leadership over the next generation should be. We must try to build a Jewish community that is not simply concerned with survival, but one that is creative and attractive to our children—a community with substance and content, a community that stresses not only memory and remembrance but also other important values of our tradition: social justice, equity, and compassion. We will need a Jewish community in Canada whose members will take pride in its activities and achievements. We will have to find ways to convert alienation to action and passivity to pride—the pride of being possessors of a great legacy, a legacy that has meaning for today and beyond.

The irony of Jewish life today is that we may be doomed by the very freedom that we fought centuries to achieve. In Canada, Jews are confronted by a classic product of a pluralistic society. We desperately want to integrate fully into a society that until recently we were not allowed into; yet we know that if we do so we may not be able to maintain ourselves as a unique, vibrant, identifiable community. Paradoxically, throughout our history, Jews have feared a truly open society as much as they desperately and valiantly fought for it. Our greatest triumph—helping to create in North America an open, democratic society—may result in our greatest defeat.

Today, Jews in North America worry more about rates of assimilation than about rates of anti-Semitism. Absorption, not anti-Semitism, seems our greatest threat in North America. Our greatest concern is for our children. Will they remain Jewish? Will our community survive into the next century as strongly as it leaves this? Are the very seeds of our destruction implanted in our success? Can Jewishness in this country survive freedom? Can it survive an open, tolerant, multicultural society?

The challenges facing Canadian Jewry are formidable. But we are a formidable people.

NOTES

1 Palmer, H. *Immigration and the Rise of Multiculturalism.* Toronto: Copp Clark Publishing, 1982.

2 *Proceedings of the Senate Committee on Immigration and Labour, 1946.* Ottawa, 1946.

3 Hawkins, Freda. "Canadian Immigration: Present Policies and Future Options". Round Table 1977, *pg. 17.*

4 *The Reid Report.* Winnipeg: Angus Reid Group, 1993.

5 *The Globe and Mail.* September 11, 1992.

[6] Elazar, David and Waller, Harold. *Maintaining Consensus: The Canadian Jewish Polity in the Postwar World.* Lanham, Md., 1990.

[7] Tulchinsky, G. "The Contours of Canadian Jewish History." *Journal of Canadian Studies,* 1982-3.

[8] Tulchinsky, G. *Taking Root: The Origins of the Canadian Jewish Community.* Toronto: 1992.

[9] Taras, David and Weinfeld, Morton. "Continuity and Criticism: North American Jews and Israel." *International Journal.* Summer 1990.

[10] Abella, Irving. *A Coat of Many Colours: Two Centuries of Jewish Life in Canada.* Toronto: 1990.

THE ROLE OF ETHNIC MINORITIES IN THE PURSUIT OF EQUALITY AND MULTICULTURALISM

Emilio S. Binavince

INTRODUCTION

Some very influential and vocal Canadians have made the indictment that multiculturalism is a heavy cross on the shoulder of the taxpayer without visible benefit to Canada and, more seriously, that it is divisive. Consequently, ethnic minorities are substantially to blame for Canada's national disintegration.

This is a bogus charge; the national disintegration of Canada is basically a French/English confrontation. The role of ethnic minorities in this unfortunate confrontation is that of a calm, dispassionate peace-keeper, occasionally a puzzled spectator. There is nothing unpatriotic in loving one's roots, valuing one's ethnic traditions, religion and language, and working to preserve them. Those who make this charge have a distorted definition of patriotism. Canada's constitution being founded on the tenets of equality and tolerance, how can we consider a commitment to one's cultural traditions as a betrayal?

THE STRUGGLE FOR EQUALITY AND MULTICULTURALISM

The ethnic community's struggle for multiculturalism and equality in the constitutional debate in the recent past testifies to the contrary. Minorities seek equality on moral grounds, nothing less and nothing more. They want equal access to government power and the institutions of government. They believe that this access begins with the Constitution. They want to find themselves in that blueprint of Canadian society. A Constitution that attempts to entrench the enshrined and stronger position of French and English Canadians while undermining equality rights would be indefensible. Constitutions are largely protective in character. They are control mechanisms against abuse of government power. The French and English majority, being in control of the government, does not need the Constitution to protect it. Those who need the Constitution for protection are those who cannot help themselves within government. Any person who has followed the constitutional history of our country and the composition of government since Confederation will immediately recognize the control English and French Canadians exert over government: they are the government, and they are the majority in Canada. Why then is it necessary to add constitutional provisions that would strengthen the position of French and English Canada? The constitutionalization of French and English rights has only emotional significance. French and English Canadians want these high sounding declarations to reassure themselves of their entrenched position of power. If they feel the need to make those declarations, then they are at liberty to do so provided that they do not constitutionalize the exclusion of ethnic communities.

Leading ethnic minority organizations have relentlessly urged governments to take specific measures for the promotion of multi-culturalism: the enactment of the Multiculturalism Act, adequate funding for the department, and the creation of the Race Relations Foundation of Canada are examples. Successive governments have not acted on the basis of principle, but on the convenience of partisan political imperative which reflects the ebb and flow of public opinion. For this reason, multiculturalism has been under siege in the last few years. Politicians and governments have to understand that multiculturalism, like equality, is not a matter of mere policy; it is a matter of constitutional right. The struggle for equality is not distinguishable from the search for Canadian multiculturalism. Multiculturalism is but the most visible aspect of equality. The driving principle behind multiculturalism for ethnic minorities is not nationalism; it is equality. A neglect or disregard of this right is actionable in court under the Charter. In my view, there is little merit to the judicial analysis that takes the Charter[1] as a catalogue of mere prohibitions (rather than directions). Such an analysis has been the foundation upon which this anaemic approach to multiculturalism has been constructed.

This position has sired unfounded fear in the minds of English and French Canadians. It has been exaggerated so as to be equated with the desire of the aboriginal people for the creation of an autonomous level of government. This is a false generalization. One cannot argue, in response to the recognition of minority languages, cultures and religions, that ethnic minorities may just as well form independent countries or societies. No member of the ethnic community has asked for an autonomous province or autonomous government. Indeed, the unmistakable objective of minorities is clear: They do not want separate homelands such as characterized the South African apartheid policy. They want to be a member of the national fabric or tapestry; they want to be a part of the national consciousness; they want to be Canadians. The modest demand for the recognition of language, for the protection of religion and equal rights in terms of access to powers, government, or education cannot be exaggerated into a demand for autonomy.

Ethnic minorities have supported a view of federalism that differs in substance from that represented by mainstream Canadians, one based on neutral principles. To them, the recurrent refrain in the constitutional debate has been the issue of power. This is a topic less urgent to the people (who are citizens of the provinces on the one hand, and citizens of Canada on the other). It is only urgent and important to politicians and power groups who govern the provinces and Canada, and to those who have an unreasoning enthusiasm for tribalism which masquerades as nationalism. Ethnic community organizations over the past several years have not argued for greater federal or provincial power merely because they believed in the principle of centralization or decentralization. Centralization and decentralization are empty words, mere incantations in this debate. If the purpose of government is to benefit the people, then the institution or level of government that can maximize the benefit to the people at the least possible cost must have the relevant powers. The task, therefore, is to find the level of government that can serve the people best. It is not useful to argue about one level of government having more power than another level of government. The function of government is not the accumulation of power *per se*. Politicians involved in constitutional law making have difficulty accepting this principle. First Ministers were asked to look at each power dispassionately and assign them according to who can exercise them best at the lowest possible cost for the benefit of Canadians. This idea minimizes the significance of the quantity of power and uses as a yardstick the only true test that performance of government is measured by. It puts serving the people at the very heart of the debate.

More significant than the allocation of power has been the demand by minorities for the abolition of the Notwithstanding Clause from the Charter. More than any provision in Canada's constitution, this provision poses the most serious threat to ethnic minorities. This clause renders meaningless—at the moment when it is most needed—the protection of the Constitution. This clause, in effect, makes most guarantees in the Constitution a matter of the grace of those who are in power—the mainstream majority—and throws this country back to the tradition that puts civil liberties within the ambit of politics. For this reason, it makes a farce of the Charter's greatest achievement: that the people have declared greater faith in the objectivity and impartiality of courts than in the vicissitudes of politics.

Consistent with our faith in Canada's commitment to fairness as reflected in the Charter, Canadians should demand popular input into the rewriting of the Constitution. Many people, particularly politicians and our elites, believe that the best procedure is to put the First Ministers in a room and let them debate the issues—horse-trade this power for that power or that right for this right. For minorities and other equality seekers this procedure is unseemly, unprincipled in the extreme. Over the years, the position of minorities has been gaining support among Canadians; the reaction of the Canadian people to the conventional process has become increasingly hostile. This hostility signals an increasing distrust of our politicians' ability to amend the Constitution. The demise of the Meech Lake Accord and the resounding rejection of the Charlottetown Accord carried this unmistakable message: The people want the job of writing the Constitution in their own hands. Canadians do not want to follow the executive model for writing a constitution; they want a constituent assembly or convention. Some people fear that it is difficult to put together a constituent assembly; the assembly might craft something that will substantially remake the Canadian confederation. To this I would reply that if the people are the repository of government powers, powers that are merely entrusted to politicians for the time being, there is nothing wrong with the people changing Canada into a form that they want. How can the trustees of power have greater legitimacy than the people from whom they derive their power?

But the most amazing thrust of this proposition is that some Third World countries, such as South Africa and the Philippines, and less educated peoples who have no long tradition in democracy have been able to write their own constitution by way of a constitutional convention. Why is that Canadians—among the best educated peoples in the world, with one of the highest standards of living, and with an established tradition of democracy—cannot be trusted to rewrite the Constitution? That, to me, is a mystifying position. I believe that the people are capable of this task. Ethnic minorities and immigrants would be glad to provide the rich experience that they bring from their countries of origin as a contribution to the reworking of the Constitution.

HIGHLIGHTS OF THE CONTRIBUTION OF ETHNIC MINORITIES IN THE CONSTITUTIONAL DEBATE SINCE 1980

Ethnic minorities had not been involved in any significant way in constitutional development before the 1980s. That is not unusual. Before the enactment of the Immigration Act of 1967, Canadian policy accepted only immigrants who were capable of being assimilated into the English or French communities. After the Second World War, the increasing number of people who were refugees and the need of Canadians to maintain their standard of living at the level reached in the war economy resulted in an open door immigration policy. That change touched a constitutional sore spot because the people who came to this country were placed according to the so-called "English conformity model". It created concern in Quebec that the increasing number of people coming to this country who ultimately became part of English Canada, would erode the status of French Canada. For ethnic communities, it was never their intention to create fear in the minds of French Canadians; it is not their intention today to create fear in Quebec. These immigrants can proudly say that they, over the past ten years, have demonstrated their passion to learn a language other than their own. Indeed, the hesitation of English Canadians to learn French or of French Canadians to learn English is absolutely puzzling to newcomers from countries where learning several languages is the norm.

In the 1980s, the Canadian Ethnocultural Council (CEC), a coalition of national ethnic organizations was organized. One of the first debates it participated in related to the drafting of the Canadian Charter of Rights and Freedoms. One of the remarkable achievements of this organization and other ethnic organizations is the inclusion of Section 27 of the

Canadian Charter of Rights and Freedoms, which reads as follows:

> *27. This Charter shall be interpreted in a manner consistent with the preservation and enhancement of the multicultural heritage of Canadians.*

It was through a considerable organizing effort that this provision was included in the Charter. Although the power of this provision remains largely untested, this provision signaled a Copernican turn in the development of a multicultural Canada.[2]

The first draft of the Charter that was tabled in the House of Commons on October 6, 1980 did not include Section 27. Representations were made before the Special Joint Committee in the House in order to have this provision included. It must be acknowledged that it was Jean Chrétien, then the Minister of Justice, who returned the draft to the House with the inclusion of Section 27. I am sure that ethnic minorities are grateful for his effort which ensured that when the new resolution was introduced in the House on November 20, 1981, Section 27 was included. However, when the First Ministers met, they removed it from the draft. Many Canadians ask why the ethnic communities do not trust the premiers of the provinces. The answer is apparent from this action; it is evidence of the lack of understanding of the ethnic community by premiers in the country. Ethnic minorities tend to trust the federal government more than they trust the provinces today largely for two reasons: the first is their record in constitutional-law making, and the second is the commitment of the federal government to immigration.

The second important episode in the struggle of ethnic minorities relates to the Meech Lake Accord. The Parti Québécois was defeated in 1985, and Brian Mulroney and the Conservative Party had taken power in 1984. The big question then was what would happen in relation to the Constitution. Robert Bourassa offered the five conditions for Quebec's acceptance of the Constitution Act of 1982. Mr. Mulroney's government was eager to please Quebec; so the Government of Canada started the discussions and negotiations that resulted in the Meech Lake Accord. This was probably one of the most difficult times for ethnic organizations because many considered the Meech Lake Accord to be inadequate and very much flawed. But the communities, and I included, were torn between opposing the Meech Lake Accord on the one hand, and becoming a factor in the breakup of this country on the other. The decision taken by the CEC and many members of the ethnic communities was clear. They were willing to close their eyes to what were considered as flaws in the Accord to help in holding this country together. George Corn, then President of the CEC, stated at the time of the Charlottetown Accord debates: "Our first duty as Canadians is the unity of the country." I, personally, did not believe that a rejection of the Meech Lake Accord would dismember the country. Nonetheless, we were and are united in the position that Canadian unity is foremost in the minds of the CEC; it is foremost in the minds of ethnic community members.

If the Meech Lake Accord, as originally proposed, had been adopted, it would have neutralized Section 27 of the Charter. The CEC and many ethnic organizations argued that the Meech Lake Accord, in articulating the fundamental characteristics of Canada, should have accorded as much recognition to multiculturalism as to linguistic duality. As redrafted in the Langevin Block and released on June 3, 1987, the Accord contained a provision, Section 16, that immunized Section 27 from the impact of the linguistic duality/distinct society clause. Nonetheless, the CEC felt that multiculturalism remained a second-class constitutional value. In the CEC's words, it "relegates multiculturalism to the back of the bus".

There were other ideas sponsored by the CEC which were crucial to multiculturalism and equality in Canada at this time. The reflection of cultural diversity in the Senate and the Courts, particularly the Supreme Court of Canada, stands prominent. But the CEC was not alone in the forefront of this struggle. The Chinese Canadian National Council, the

German-Canadian National Congress, the National Association of Japanese Canadians and the Ukrainian Canadian Committee were active as well.

The Accord failed to get ratification in the required three-year period. Many were saddened by the demise of Meech Lake, but there were those of us who looked at it as a new challenge for an innovative round of constitutional law making. The governments of the provinces and the federal government created committees, commissions, and task forces in order to elicit proposals relating to the constitution. Many ethnic organizations, national and local, and many individuals, appeared before these committees in order to contribute ideas. A number were consulted by the Citizens' Forum on Canada's Future, otherwise known as the Spicer Commission. The CEC appeared before the Beaudoin-Edwards Committee to discuss the amending procedure. The Castonguay-Dobbie Special Committee on a Renewed Canada made recommendations which reflected some of the ethnic community's concerns. With the appointment of Joe Clark as Constitutional Affairs Minister, the officials of the CEC directed their efforts to persuading Mr. Clark and his staff.

On August 27 and 28, 1992, the First Ministers and the representatives of the territories and of the aboriginal peoples authored the Charlottetown Accord. The writing of Charlottetown was indicative of the lack of seriousness accorded to minorities. The Charlottetown Accord is historical evidence of how the mainstream interest groups who control the country ignored neutral principles and gave weight to power politics. Ethnic minorities found themselves looking in from the outside, not invited to be observers in the process. They had to resort to subterfuge just to be bystanders—by becoming a part of the Native Council of Canada. It is unseemly to pretend that we are members of those honoured Canadians who can justly claim to be the first inhabitants of this land. In spite of the fact that ethnic minorities were in Charlottetown not so much with a long shopping list of powers, but to assist in the discussions and to clarify issues, we had to wear a face quite different from our own just to be observers. And the question we may ask ourselves for years to come is why governments, negotiators and politicians doubted the ability of ethnic communities to contribute to a meaningful discussion of the Constitution. The reason is that they did not like the equality rights that minorities and other equality seeking groups have espoused. It seems as if the entrenched power elites of Canada wanted to have a vertical mosaic in Canada, where ethnic minorities would rank lower than others.

Many in the ethnic community, myself included, were not persuaded that fear of national disintegration was a valid reason to support a flawed constitutional document known as the Charlottetown Accord. The majority of Canadians, including francophones in Quebec, anglophones in the West and aboriginal peoples, decisively disagreed with their leaders. There has never been a more resounding message that the people do not want their leaders horse-trading on the Constitution.

CONCLUSION

What assessment may one make of the contribution of ethnic minorities in the multicultural and constitutional movement? Sadly, I have to conclude that if one draws the line and adds up the numbers, we have only one real, lasting achievement: Section 27. This is a fragile achievement. The life of Section 27 of the Charter is precarious today in the hands of the courts. Our enormous efforts in constitutional debate have not, therefore, been crowned with achievement. They have not produced any great tangible result because our objectives have not been properly understood. As to multiculturalism, our achievement is even more precarious. There are those in the ethnic community, like Neil Bissondath, who have been converted to the cynical view that multiculturalism and substantive equality are a radicalism destructive of Canada.

Achievement is beyond our grasp as long as minorities are divided and not persuaded of the fairness and merit of our cause. In this regard, we need a new strategy to mobilize these Canadians. Further, minorities have to stress to political leaders and other Canadians that our efforts are not driven by a will to get power or special protection. The community must, in the future, be more aggressive in making itself heard. It can contribute creatively to Canada in the multicultural and constitutional debate.

NOTES

1 See my "Democracy and the Accountability of the Judges for Charter Decisions", in *Taking Stock: The Jurisprudence on the Charter and Minority Rights.* Ottawa: Canadian Ethnocultural Council, pp. vi-ix.

2 For an excellent survey of the cases, see Gerald Gall, "Multiculturalism and *The Canadian Charter of Rights and Freedoms*: The Jurisprudence to Date under Section 27" in *Taking Stock: The Jurisprudence on the Charter and Minority Rights,* pp. 73-112.

OUR CONSTITUTION DOES NOT ADMIT OF DISTINCTIONS OR RACES

Nathan M. Greenfield

Following my talk at the Juliet Cuenco Annual Memorial Seminar (May, 1996) during which I argued that by becoming racialist and clientalist, Canada's multicultural policy has weakened Canadian citizenship, a defender of the policy told me that to "deal with her", I would have to "deal" with her "brown skin". Had she been, say, a Muslim and claimed that to deal with her I would have to at some level deal with Islam, I would have agreed; offering her a ham sandwich or defaming the Prophet would have been boorish.

But her brown skin had no such clear meaning, though I knew what she wanted it to mean. She wanted her "brown skin" *to be* the history of slavery and racism, a record of (what I agree is) the sin of "the West". Since I'm caucasian and caucasians enslaved and oppressed people of colour, "dealing" with her means "dealing with" (expatiating?) this history.

I'm sorry, but I can't.

It's not that I deny history. Indeed, my doctoral thesis argues that the American "negro" author Charles W. Chesnutt deserves an honoured place in the canon.[1] I've even lived some history while working to desegregate Boston's public schools. And it's not even that, as my surname indicates, I too could reach for the laurel of most historically oppressed.

No, the reason why I can't make a big "deal" over skin colour is because to do so would be to dishonour Cora Elder of Brooklyn, New York, the woman who all but raised my brother and me and who is my son's godmother. You see, when I was in second grade, I once joked that Cora "was born someplace out in the sun", and my mother washed my mouth out with soap.

THE PROBLEM WITH RACIAL THINKING

Every speaker at the conference was a "new Canadian". But, it fell to me, the newest, to point out that anti-racism, the most important component of multiculturalism, is much older than the Secretariat created by an Order-in-Council drafted by Pierre Trudeau. Indeed, Canadians embraced multiculturalism, the charter and just this year rejected Reform MP Bob Ringma's musings about restricting "gays and Blacks . . . to the back of the shop" because our constitution, both the legal one and the one Canadian citizens carry around in their heads, "does not admit of distinctions of races or classes".[2]

My claim is not, of course, that our national escutcheon is unstained. It is, by:

- the treatment of Canada's native peoples;
- anti-French attitudes of Orange Ontario and the West, which in the language of the day had as much to do with race as it did with language and religion;
- the head tax placed on Asian immigrants;

- the treatment of Canadians of German origin during World War I, an example conveniently left off most lists of "oppression";
- the treatment of Canadians of Japanese origin during World War II;
- the "none is too many" policy vis-à-vis Jews fleeing Hitler;
- the destruction of Africville;
- the segregation of some schools in Nova Scotia and Ontario.

But our national history also includes:

- Lord Simcoe's act to end slavery in 1793 (four years after the United States' Constitution protected it);
- Lord Chief Justice Monk's 1798 declaration that slavery did not exist in Quebec;
- the refuge given to some 30,000 slaves who fled to freedom on the underground railroad;
- Mr. Justice Archibald's ruling in *Johnson v. Sparrow et al.* (1899) that the Academy of Music in Montreal could not refuse to sit a black couple that had purchased tickets.[3]
- *The Insurance Act of Ontario* of 1932 (which made discriminating "because of race" in the provision of insurance illegal);
- *The Unemployment Relief Act* of 1933;
- Ontario's *Racial Discrimination Act* of 1944;
- an incident that prompted a Louisville reporter to write—when Jackie Robinson ran from a Montreal crowd in 1947—"It was the first time a black man ran from a crowd with love rather than hate on its mind." This, while Billy Holliday sang of "Strange Fruit on Southern Trees";
- Saskatchewan's *Bill of Rights Act* of 1947;
- Ontario's *Fair Employment Practices Act* of 1954.

We dismantled racial immigration restrictions in the 1960's and early 70's, before even Gage heard of multiculturalism. Canada accepted the highest number of Vietnamese “boat-people”—and, unlike the Hungarian Refugees of ’56, they weren't Caucasians.

A “woman of colour” sits at the federal cabinet table. A “man of colour” is Chief of the Federal Court and one has served as Ontario's Lieutenant Governor. A descendant of Asiatics served as Lieutenant Governor of British Columbia; another sits at the federal cabinet table. There are at least two persons of colour in the Senate, and last time I looked, not even the Reform Party made an issue of their skin colour. Their party affiliation, yes; their melanin content, no.

More is at stake in this last paragraph than makes me comfortable. For with it, I've taken the first step toward accepting (as the grounds for political analysis) what I believe to be the greatest threats to citizenship in my new country: racial thinking and clientalism. Racial thinking—let's be honest, *blood thinking*—used to be the preserve of White Supremacists who believed that “one drop of nigger blood makes a man a nigger.”[4] In 1901, Canadian Census authorities declared that “children begotten of marriages of whites and one of the other races will be classified as red, black or yellow. . .irrespective of their degree of colour.”

A half-century after the defeat of the Nazis, everybody's playing cards have only one suit: racial difference. Professor Leonard Jefferies of the City College of New York argues that “white men” are evil because they lack melanin. Ontario's schools have programs to “develop” students' “pride in their racial/ethnocultural identity and heritage”, an innoxious enough concept until one remembers that “pride” in “your” race is almost always accompanied by disdain for others' and as long as one doesn't ask the difficult question: “How do we determine race?”

I hasten to add that informing students—all students, of all cultures—about the achievements of different ethnic, cultural and historical groups is laudable. Students should be taught to take pride in the achievements of the human race, of all of our ancestors. And, they should be taught that all of them made mistakes. Hagiography is fine in religion; it has no place in a public curriculum.

Unfortunately, a government approved method is at the ready. Ironically, at the very same time anthropologists like Professors Bernard Trigger (McGill) are saying that "if you walked from Norway to West Africa, mile by mile people would get a little darker. . . .But there's nowhere you could draw a line and say, 'These people are white and these people are black'."

THE IMPOSSIBILITY OF DEFINING RACE

Statistics Canada has produced an algebra that determines race. At first glance, the algebra, unveiled in the May 1996 census (Question 19 of the long form), seems to take into account Trigger's point. Instead of the usual four races, StatsCan now recognizes at least ten and even allows for multiple assignation. However, unlike Question 17, which asked "To which ethnic or *cultural group(s)* did this person's ancestors belong" (e.g. French, English, Somali, Jewish), Question 19 asked "*Is this person*: White, Chinese, South Asian, Black, Arab/West African, Filipino, South East Asian, Latin-American, Japanese, Korean or Other?" (Emphasis mine.) Our national bean counters' confusion of race, nationality and geography is nothing less than astounding.

StatsCan didn't ask about race. It didn't have to. Anyone who received the long form knows that any list that begins with "White" and which contains "Black" is asking about *race*. Had I answered the question, my personal blood line would have become a statement with public policy implications. As I did on my census form, I'd like to indicate that I refused to answer Question 19 and thus have not complied fully with the act under which the census is collected.

Far from taking into account Trigger's point, what the list accompanying Question 19 takes into account is raw politics. In 1986, North Africans were "Black"; now they are "Arabs". Cubans and Puerto Ricans, who used to be "Black", are now "Latin Americans". Filipinos got their own category in 1986, after co-habitating in the (Rogers and Hammerstein?) category of "countries often visualized and portrayed as exotic islands in the Pacific." These changes had nothing to do with anthropology. Rather, a group's appearance or movement depends upon how StatsCan responded to pressures from ethno/cultural interest groups.

THE PRACTICE OF "REVERSE DISCRIMINATION"

Here, appearances count. Although StatsCan hides it beneath the bureaucratic language of the note accompanying Question 19—"This information is collected to support programs which promote equal opportunity for everyone to share in the social, cultural and economic life of Canada"—the reason why StasCan is interested in race is because of employment equity. Employment equity is less a program dedicated to rooting out racist hiring practices—such a program would use "sting" operations like those being used in the United States to enforce fair housing legislation—than it is a belief that Canadian society is (almost) irredeemably racist and that the labour market should be re-ordered along clientalist lines.

The Abella Report (1984) failed to provide any Canadian figures to support the claim that "visible minorities" had been systematically excluded from the labour market. The authors of the Employment Equity Act (1986) assumed they had been and set up machinery designed to raise representation of "designated groups" to pre-set targets, generally their percentage distribution in the labour market.

Interestingly enough, StatsCan reported in 1986 that there was little difference between the earnings of those *StatsCan identified* as visible minorities born in Canada and non-visible minority Canadians. Canadians of Japanese origin are second only to Jewish Canadians. Canadians of Portuguese extraction underperform Jamaican Canadians, who are tied with Greek Canadians.

Under employment equity, what matters is not that there are poor Canadians who need help, training or even protection. What matters is that certain ethnocultural groups—let's be blunt again, *racial* groups—have staked claim to jobs for their members. What matters is not that there are jobs and people vying to fill them. What matters is skin colour, and *volk*.

The Royal Canadian Mounted Police has not established separate hiring targets for applicants from different income groups. Neither has the Ottawa Fire Department established separate hiring targets for good looking or ugly men and women, though a mountain of studies has shown that the "halo-affect" determines success in job interviews and advancement. No. Both have separate lists for "visible minority" and other Canadians based solely on race.

Ontario's recently repealed Employment Equity Act (Bill-79) would have forced companies with more than 50 employees to hire so that their workforces mirrored the percentage each government-identified ethnocultural (racial) group had in the province—actually, in Toronto. Exactly why anyone would believe that all things being equal, every workplace would mirror society has never been explained. The office charged with implementing Bill-79 contained exactly one able-bodied white male.

Employment equity's supporters claim that such measures are needed to ensure a "level playing field" today. Those who admit that percentage hiring or preferential hiring might disadvantage whites who are applying for jobs today, justify this by citing group rights and historical group disadvantages. At an abstract level, both defenses hold water.

But we don't live at an abstract level. We live today in a democratic polity which grants each Canadian equal rights. To distribute jobs on the basis of race is *clientalist* and as such is worthy of a Boston ward healer and not of a mature democracy. Likewise, to turn a blind eye to discrimination is immoral and not the Canadian way. As Mr. Justice Archibald wrote in *Sparrow* in 1901:

> *Our constitution is and always has been essentially democratic, and it does not admit of distinctions of races or classes. All men are equal before the law and each has equal rights as a member of* ***the*** *community. . . . I should certainly hold any regulation which deprived negroes as a class of privileges which all other members of the community had a right to demand was not only unreasonable but entirely incompatible with our free democratic institutions.* (Emphasis mine.)

We cannot preserve—nay, improve—on them by defining Canadians on the basis of their pigmentation any more than we can on their religion.

To those, like the respondent at the conference who said that my views are too utopian, that the only way to fight racism is by using racial differences to even things out, I respond: In a democracy you can't. Racist hiring or renting practices are illegal; let us treat them as such and bring the cases. If those aggrieved feel unable, let the human rights commissions set up sting operations.

But, to ask me to say that race is a marker, that skin colour has meaning, is to ask me to dishonour both Cora and those who have fought for a colour blind society.

NOTES

[1] Greenfield, Nathan M. "'Their position[s] must be mined': Charles W. Chesnutt's Assault on Racial Thinking". Dissertation, McGill University, Montreal, 1994.

Technically speaking, Chesnutt was a "mulatto"; however, fin de siècle Americans believed in the "one drop" rule. Hence, he was considered "coloured", "negro", "African-American", and "Afro-American", each of which he used. His attitude toward race is best summed up by the question: "Why should a man be proud [of his race] any more than he should be ashamed of anything for which he is not responsible?", and the claim that he asks for himself and for all "a manly self-respect based upon one's humanity, a self-respect which claims nothing for colour and yields nothing to colour."

Chesnutt travelled through Southern Ontario in the late 1890's and recorded that he found it a pleasant place.

[2] Mr. Justice Archibald in *Johnson v. Sparrow et al.*, Montreal, 1899.

[3] At the Juliet Cuenco Seminar (May, 1996), another panelist argued that Sparrow does not support the claim that Canadian law has an "anti-racist" streak. Oddly, he didn't stake this claim on the fact that *Sparrow* was ignored by subsequent courts. Rather, he argued that because Mr. Justice Archibald decided Sparrow on the basis of contract law (the ticket being a contract), it was solely a business decision.

My view is that contract law has been one of the most effective ways of expanding rights. The interstate bus boycotters in the American South pointed out that the United States federal government had the power to ban discrimination because the United States Constitution gave

---

it power over Interstate Commerce, in other words, over interstate contracts. The United States Supreme Court has cited this power more often than any other to support civil rights legislation.

4 For a full discussion of the "one drop" rule see George M. Frederickson's *The Black Image in the White Mind: The Debate on Afro-American Character and Destiny, 1817-1914,* New York: Harper, 1974.

TRUE NORTH STRONG AND HYPHEN-FREE

R.L. Gabrielle Nishiguchi

The bilingual, multicultural union which we recognize as Canada rests unperturbed beneath a Damoclean sword of potentially huge dimensions. Who would have thought that an enormous threat could turn on a little "line" of truly remarkable mien: the humble hyphen?

With each passing decade since sharing in the 1945 triumph of the United Nations, Canadians continue to search with increasing urgency for ways in which to cross lines of colour, culture and religion. Yet the more we criss-cross these lines which establish our identity, the more it becomes apparent that the very lines that define us also confine us. In 1975, former Progressive Conservative Prime Minister John George Diefenbaker admonished and challenged us to have vision: "One Canada, one nation, my Canada, your Canada, cannot be a hyphenated Canada."[1] However, the hyphen remains and so do the prefixes. This nation's psychological horizon is peopled with French-Canadians, Japanese-Canadians, English-Canadians, Jewish-Canadians, Aboriginal-Canadians and Jamaican-Canadians—to name only a few of the ethnic stocks our beleagured body politic is heir to. Why won't this tenacious *tiret* go away? Or perhaps more to the point, why won't we let it go?

During the Royal Commission on Bilingualism and Biculturalism, Commissioner André Laurendeau mused in his diary about being "Canadian" during the sixties: "When one examines it more closely, it usually means an English Canadian, who agrees to set aside a little space for Quebec, but who at the same time is upset by having to say so."[2] Thirty years later, one can easily exchange the word "Quebec" for any of our hyphenated minorities. In principle, most everyone agrees that there is enough space in our concept of Canada to accommodate a multitude of races and religions. Still, as Laurendeau wryly observed, resentment does arise when we have to "say so" or when we find ourselves actually having to set aside space – job, living or recreational – for an unfamiliar ethnic face attached to an unpronounceable surname, doing unfamiliar things.

What can we do? Surrendering a hyphen is one thing. But are we ready to erase the most divisive of lines: the line separating our image of the ideal Canadian face from that of the unfamiliar "other"? And there's the rub. If truth be told, the operative word in the business of being Canadian really isn't multi*culturalism*, it's multi*facialism.* (One suspects that is what riled Jacques Parizeau and Bernard Landry on Referendum night in October 1995: the image of all those ethnic faces belonging to the "other" halting the Parti Québecois advance on *indépendance*.) In short, compressed within the ubiquitous hyphen—that tiny splash of ink uniting words but distancing worlds—lies the unhappy legacy of the "other" Canadian. While the physical mark of punctuation can be deleted with a backspace button, its unyielding psychological baggage, bound with the heavy straps of history and memory, cannot be jettisoned with quite so much dispatch.

Does it matter? History shows us that it does and that the human price alone should make hyphen-hunting a priority. The treatment of Canadians of Japanese descent, both during and immediately after the Second World War, is a case in point. The community's mass evacuation, internment, dispossession, and dispersion culminated in 1946 with the deportation of 3,964 of the most vulnerable to war-devastated Japan. This deplorable record has attracted much attention over the past 10 to 15 years. But, perhaps even more illuminating is to look into the archival record for documents which help us see "hyphenated thought" in action.

In 1942, faced with the problem of what sort of bedding should be issued to evacuees, straw paillasses were selected because the Minister of Labour Humphrey Mitchell felt "the Japanese in their own mode of life were not used to spring beds or pillows".[3] The damp straw aggravated an already miserable infestation problem. Canadian-born children, who had indeed known the comfort of beds in their pre-war life, "took it for granted that in the morning we would wake up covered with bedbug bites",[4] recalls veteran scientist-broadcaster, Dr. David Suzuki. Mitchell and many of his Cabinet colleagues were simply unable to see the Canadian lurking behind the Japanese prefix.

Over a half century later, we still suffer from a Mitchell-like myopia. We don't see the Canadian speaking the words, because to see the Canadian would mean obliterating the line between "us" and the "other". And it is in this context that Japanese Canadian Redress is best understood. When Progressive Conservative Prime Minister Brian Mulroney announced the Redress Settlement in Parliament on September 22, 1988, what he really said to a deeply wounded community was: "We made a mistake. We thought you were Japanese, but today we acknowledge you were and are Canadians." What he said to this nation was: "We are Canadians, true north strong and hyphen-free."

In May 1932, Canada's thirty-fifth Governor General, Lord Tweedsmuir, exhorted his audience to hold fast to their old traditions, but to face the future with "clear candid eyes".[5] We need those eyes now more than ever: to see Canadians first and last. Strangely enough, in the unity game, it just may be that, against the chaos of *multifacialism*, the best way to draw the line is to withdraw it.

NOTES

1 Diefenbaker, John George. *One Canada: The Memoirs of the Rt. Honourable John G. Diefenbaker, The Crusading Years (1895-1956).* Scarborough: MacMillan-NAL Publishing, 1975, p. 202.

2 *The Diary of André Laurendeau (1964-67).* Translated by Patricia Smart and Dorothy Howard. Toronto: James Lorimer & Co., 1991, p. 49.

3 *RG 22, Volume 740, U2000, Memorandum for File, Conference in Humphrey Mitchell's Office, 30 March 1942.* National Archives of Canada.

4 Suzuki, David. *Metamorphosis: Stages in a Life.* Toronto: Stoddart Publishing, 1941, pp. 13-14.

5 Lord Tweedsmuir. *Canadian Occasions.* Toronto: The Musson Book Company, 1941, pp. 13-14.

NEW RACISM, CULTURAL DIVERSITY AND THE SEARCH FOR A NATIONAL IDENTITY

Li Zong

Despite the Canadian Charter of Rights and the multiculturalism policy, the dramatic influx of refugees and immigrants from the Third World and a large volume of business immigrants from Asian countries have produced renewed racial attitudes and a resurgence of racism in Canada in recent years. This paper examines the formation and characteristics of what may be called "new racism", and analyzes its ideological basis.

EMERGENCE OF NEW RACISM AND ITS FEATURES

Racism has been generated and reproduced within complex historical and social contexts. Before World War II, overt racism based on the belief in racial superiority was dominant in Europe and North America. It was widely accepted that the Caucasian "race" was physically and genetically superior to other races, and was characterized by an inherent capacity for freedom and an ability to create democratic institutions, capacities which they could impose in many other parts of the world (Horsman, 1976, 1981: 9-77; MacDougall, 1982). With the expansion of capitalism and colonialism, the "innate superiority" of Whites and the "natural inferiority" of Blacks and other non-white peoples have been used to legitimate and justify racial oppression. Racism arose from initial unequal relationships as a dominant group sought to subjugate a subordinate group for the purpose of acquiring land, resources or cheap labour. In Canada, racism was maintained towards racialized minorities such as the Aboriginal peoples and Asian immigrants; discriminatory laws, programs, and policies were entrenched in a social order that made prejudicial views appear as though they were natural and justifiable (Zong, 1994).

After World War II, many changes contributed to the weakening of notions of racial superiority or inferiority based on biological and genetic factors. These changes include the struggle against colonial rule, the rise of nationalism, the development of sciences, and the abrogation of discriminatory laws and policies in many advanced capitalist countries. Thus, overt racism has become less acceptable in western societies. The traditional idea of genetic inferiority or superiority may still be important in the fabric of racism (Duster, 1990), but the discourse of racial inferiority is increasingly reformulated as cultural deficiency, social inadequacy, and technological underdevelopment (Rodney, 1982). An example is cultural ethnocentrism, which is a tendency to evaluate minorities' cultures on the basis of the dominant group's imposed standards (Li, 1994b). According to a survey conducted by the Angus Reid Group in February, 1989, about 13 per cent of Canadians can be considered as "ethnocentrists," based on their negative attitudes towards immigrants and refugees. The basis of these negative attitudes appeared to be largely cultural, as those expressing them were concerned with a threat to Canadian culture that they saw as coming from an emphasis on multiculturalism and from a rapidly changing population resulting from high immigration levels (Angus Reid Group, 1989: 7-8). In recent years, many scholars in North America (Elliott and Fleras, 1992; Gaertner and Dovidio, 1986; Henry et al., 1995; Katz et al., 1986; McConohay, 1986; Weigel and Howes, 1985) have drawn attention to the emergence of a form of racism in contemporary social settings which can be described as new racism.

According to Weigel and Howes (1985), the new racism is a contemporary expression of hostility towards racial minorities that goes undetected by conventional measures. The new racism often contains an oblique attack on visible minorities in a covert or disguised form. Different from the past when blatant and stereotypic forms of prejudice and discrimination were routinely directed at racial minorities with explicit hatred, the new racism usually disguises racist attitudes through behaviours that appear non-prejudicial or discriminatory on the surface. To avoid embarrassing situations or possible physical or legal retaliation, racism now is usually expressed in somewhat more muted or polite tones that are less likely to provoke outrage or indignation. Some scholars (Elliott and Fleras, 1992; Henry et al., 1995) suggest that this new racism reflects a conflict of interest between opposing values in Canadian society. "On the one hand is a commitment to abstract equality and justice (egalitarianism); on the other, an equal but often conflicting endorsement of meritocracy and universalism (individualism)". (Elliott and Fleras, 1992: 60)

IDEOLOGICAL BASIS OF NEW RACISM

Since World War II, Canada has witnessed the abolition of overt exclusionary policies and laws such as the repeal of the Chinese Immigration Act in 1947, the adoption of multiculturalism policy in 1971, and constitutional guarantees of individual rights and freedoms in 1982. These changes help to promote a democratic and tolerant society, and the value of equality in Canadian society is widely propagated. However, economic, political, and social inequalities along racial and ethnic lines still exist, and covert expressions of bigotry and stereotyping remain (Bolaria and Li, 1988; Satzewich, 1992). The contradiction between democratic principles and racial inequalities at the structural level is reflected in the conflict between the egalitarian values of justice and racist attitudes. This is the basis of what Henry et al. (1995) call "democratic racism". According to Henry et al. (1995), democratic racism is a new ideology held by the public in contemporary Canadian society "in which two conflicting sets of values are made congruent to each other. Commitments to democratic principles such as justice, equality, and fairness conflict but coexist with attitudes and behaviours that include negative feelings about minority groups and differential treatment of and discrimination against them." (Henry, et al., 1995: 21)

A survey I conducted in Vancouver in 1995[1] confirms the coexistence of these contradictory values in the public, and the findings demonstrate the basis of a new ideology shared by many respondents in their attitudes towards Chinese immigrants (see Table 1).

Table 1 shows that about 73% of the 778 adults sampled feel that there is a tension between Chinese immigrants and white Canadians in Vancouver. The tension is brought about by the presence and influx of a large volume of recent Chinese immigrants, including many business immigrants and investors moving into Vancouver. Conflicts arise over real estate, education, and other public concerns (Wong and Netting, 1992). Although people generally accept the value of racial equality, many are not prepared to accept non-white immigrants such as Chinese. As Table 1 shows, 79% of the respondents agree that "immigrants should have exactly the same job opportunities as Canadians", and 82% of the respondents agree that "minority groups in Canada should have equal opportunity for occupation, education, and promotion in society". However, European immigrants and Chinese immigrants are not equally supported by the public. There are about 73% of respondents who support admitting more European immigrants, while only about 47% of respondents support admitting more Chinese immigrants.

Table 1

	% responses		
A. Democratic Values			
1. Do you agree or disagree that immigrants should have exactly the same job opportunities as Canadians?	Agree 79.3	Disagree 19	No Answer 1.7
2. Do you agree or disagree with the statement that minority groups in Canada should have equal opportunity for occupation, education, and promotion in society?	Agree 82.1	Disagree 17.4	No Answer 0.5
B. Attitudes Towards Chinese Immigrants			
1. Are you in support of or opposed to Canada admitting more immigrants from Europe?	Support 73	Oppose 24	No Answer 2.3
2. Are you in support of or opposed to Canada admitting more immigrants from China, Taiwan and Hong Kong?	Support 47.2	Oppose 50	No Answer 2.8
3 Do you feel that there is a tension between Chinese immigrants and white Canadians in Vancouver?	Yes 72.6	No 24.8	No Answer 2.6

As the following section shows, the negative attitudes towards Chinese immigrants is not so much based on colour or biological differences, but on perceived cultural differences.

CULTURAL DIVERSITY AND NATIONAL UNITY

Since the implementation of multiculturalism policy in 1971, there has been a debate on whether or not multiculturalism promotes national unity in Canada. While Canadians generally support the values of equality and democracy, many have exhibited a remarkable degree of intolerance towards the increased presence of visible minorities in Canadian society. Some believe that different cultures brought by immigrants undermine the national unity. The 1995 Vancouver survey showed that about 50 per cent of respondents disagree with the statement that "the establishment of multiculturalism policy has promoted a democratic and tolerant society in Canada." Many people in the survey argued that multiculturalism encourages cultural diversity and denies the existence of Canadian culture, and therefore creates and reinforces separateness and racial conflict. This concern is reflected in public attitudes towards recent Chinese immigrants in Vancouver. The following are some comments made by respondents in the 1995 Vancouver survey:

> *Less emphasis should be placed on a multiculturalism policy. Effort and funds should go towards emphasising assimilation into the Canadian way of life as my family did 90 years ago.* (Male of German origin, age 59)

> *"Multiculturalism" should be replaced by a new goal "Uniculturalism". The old saying applies: "United we stand divided we fall."* (Male of British origin, age 73)

> *I am against any individualised multiculturalism. Canada is a country with two cultures (English and French). Any other immigrants of other culture have to adjust. Only by way of assimilation can Canada become one nation.* (Female of German origin, age 79)

> *English is the language of this country. To learn English is part of the deal in coming here. It is offensive how young Chinese openly flaunt*

their disregard for the English-speaking population. (Female of German origin, age 72)

Immigrants should be prepared to adapt to the Canadian way of life—become Canadians. They should not expect Canada or Canadians to adapt to them. (Female of British origin, age 60)

I believe that Chinese immigrants should make (a) real effort in not only adopting but rather integrating their culture with other Canadian cultures and respect other cultures and stop imposing their own standards and creating Chinese ghettos. It is also unfortunate that most of them can hardly speak English, reducing their degree of interaction with other cultures. (Male of French origin, age 49)

Part of the Chinese-Canadian conflict exists because of the attitude of "non-integration" that the Chinese community often holds; they have no reason to attempt to enter into any activities relating to Canadian culture when their community is self-contained. I would like to see Chinese make an honest effort towards learning English. (Male of British origin, age 19)

I think multiculturalism creates friction and intolerance. This is Canada and everything Canadian must and should be promoted to create unity. (Male of Dutch origin, age 53)

These comments by respondents reflect the common belief still held by many Canadians that Anglo-Saxon culture as Canadian culture is the basis of national unity in this country, and that immigrants must make conscious efforts to become "Canadian" by accepting and adopting behaviours of the dominant group. Most people would deny that race is important and almost unanimously would condemn racism as being wrong. In the 1995 Vancouver survey, about 59 per cent of respondents think that ethnic origin should not be used as a criterion in admitting immigrants to Canada, and over 82 per cent of respondents agree that minority groups in Canada should have equal opportunity for occupation, education, and promotion in society. Yet, at the same time, many people accept visible minorities and immigrants only on the basis that they can adapt to Anglo Canadian culture. The same survey shows that about 59 per cent of respondents agree that "Chinese immigrants should adapt themselves to Canadian culture in order to become real Canadian Canadians."

Cultural diversity has always been a part of Canadian society. It is an existing fact of life, and not something that can be changed artificially. Despite cultural differences, different racial and ethnic groups in Canadian society share core values such as democracy and equality. Some scholars (Breton, 1984; Li, 1994b; Mercer, 1995) suggest that although there is no empirical evidence to indicate that immigrants and their cultural diversity are posing any real threat to the dominant culture of Canada, visible minorities and "immigrants are often perceived as undermining a British-dominated traditional symbolic order, on the grounds that visible minorities are seen as carriers of foreign cultures and norms which are believed to be different, if not incompatible, with the Canadian heritage and core values." (Li, 1996: 24) As Li (1996: 23) points out:

> *the apparent growth of opposition to increased immigration to Canada and the intensification of negative sentiments towards immigrants, especially those from non-European origins, stem from the* ***perceived*** *threat to an established symbolic order and status hierarchy that are distinctly British dominated, and not necessarily from real conflicts between core Canadian values and the normative and linguistic diversities that recent immigrants are supposedly to have imported with them.*

Culture is dynamic and complex. The notion of "Anglo-Saxon Canadian culture" is vague and ambiguous, and the concept of "acculturation" or "assimilation" stressed in national unity is misleading and ill-defined. Assimilation implies that there are certain objective and widely agreed upon standards of behaviour that are indicative of social and structural integration. However, in practice, it is unclear what types of behaviour indicate a person is assimilated.

CULTURAL DIVERSITY AND CONFLICT

Cultural diversity does not in itself create racial tension and conflict. It is differential power and unequal treatments that produce racial tension or conflict. Members of the dominant group often use their "standards" as a frame of reference for interpreting and evaluating behaviours of other groups. As Elliott and Fleras (1992: 55) point out:

> *Not surprisingly, these groups are rated inferior, backward, or irrational. It can be seen that although favouritism towards one's own group can promote cohesion and morale, it can also contribute to intergroup tension and hostility, ... [and] to a proliferation of stereotypes about outgroup members.*

Finally, regarding multiculturalism policy, the real issue is not whether it harms or enhances national unity, but how it promotes mutual understanding and respectful relationships among different racial groups, and how it achieves a national solidarity and harmony within a culturally diversified society.

CONCLUSION

This paper indicates that there are contradictory social values within a multicultural society which become an important ideological basis of new racism. On the one hand, people generally accept "racial equality" and "democracy" as central values in a democratic society. On the other hand, cultural ethnocentrism prevails in society as reflected in negative attitudes towards visible minorities and immigrants. This paper criticizes the discourse that suggests cultural diversity threatens national unity and argues that national unity can be achieved in the context of cultural diversity.

REFERENCES

Angus Reid Group. *Immigration to Canada: Aspects of Public Opinion.* Winnipeg: Angus Reid Group, 1989.

Bolaria, B. S. and P. S. Li. *Racial Oppression in Canada, 2nd ed.* Toronto: Garamond Press, 1988.

Breton, Raymond. "The production and allocation of symbolic resources: an analysis of the linguistic and ethnocultural fields in Canada" in *Canadian Review of Sociology and Anthropology,* Vol. 21, no. 2, 1984, pp. 123-144.

Elliot, Jean Leonard and Augie Fleras. *Unequal Relations: An Introduction to Race and Ethnic Dynamics in Canada.* Scarborough: Prentice-Hall Canada Inc., 1992.

Essed, Philomena. *Understanding Everyday Racism: An Interdisciplinary Theory.* Newbury Park: SAGE Publications, 1991.

Gaertner, Samuel L. and John F. Dovidio. "The aversive form of racism" in *Prejudice, Discrimination, and Racism.* John Dovidio and Samuel L. Gaertner, eds. New York: Academic Press, 1986, pp. 61-90.

Henry, Frances, Tarol Tator, Winston Mattis, and Tim Rees. *The Colour of Democracy: Racism in Canadian Society.* Toronto: Harcourt Brace and Company, 1995.

Horsman, R. "Origins of racial Anglo-Saxonism in Great Britain before 1850" in *Journal of the History of Ideas,* Vol. 37, no. 3, 1976, pp. 387-410.

Idem. *Race and Manifest Destiny.* Cambridge: Harvard University Press, 1991.

Katz, Irwin, Joyce Wackenhut, and R. Glen Hass. "Racial ambivalence, value duality, and behaviour" in *Prejudice, Discrimination, and Racism.* John Dovidio and Samuel L. Gaertner, eds. New York: Academic Press, 1986, pp. 35-60.

Li, Peter S. "Unneighbourly house or unwelcome Chinese: the social construction of race in the battle over 'monster homes' in Vancouver, Canada" in *International Journal of Comparative Race and Ethnic Studies,* Vol. 1, no. 1, 1994a, pp. 14-33.

Idem. "A world apart: the multicultural world of visible minorities and the art world of Canada" in *The Canadian Review of Sociology and Anthropology,* Vol. 31, no. 4, 1994b, pp. 365-391.

Idem, *Literature Review on Immigration: Sociological Perspectives.* Ottawa: Citizenship and Immigration Canada, 1996.

MacDougall, H. A. *Racial Myth in English History: Trojans, Teutons and Anglo-Saxons.* Montreal: Harvest House, 1982.

McConohay, John B. "Modern racism, ambivalence, and the modern racism scale" in *Prejudice, Discrimination, and Racism,* John Dovidio and Samuel L. Gaertner, eds. New York: Academic Press, 1986, pp. 91-126.

Mercer, John. "Canadian cities and their immigrants: new realities" in *Annals of the American Academy of Political and Social Science,* Vol. 538, 1995, pp. 169-184.

Rodney, W. *How Europe Underdeveloped Africa.* Washington: Howard University Press, 1982.

Satzewich, Vic, ed. *Deconstructing A Nation: Immigration, Multiculturalism, and Racism in '90s Canada.* Halifax: Fernwood Publishing, 1992.

Weigel, Russel H. and Paul W. Howes. "Conceptions of racial prejudice: symbolic racism reconsidered" in *Journal of Social Issues,* Vol. 41, no. 3, 1985, pp. 117-138.

Wong, Lloyd L. and Nancy S. Netting. "Business immigration to Canada: social impact and racism" in *Deconstructing A Nation: Immigration, Multiculturalism and Racism in '90s Canada.* Vic Satzewich, ed. Halifax: Fernwood Publishing, 1992.

Zong, Li. "Structural and psychological dimensions of racism" in *Canadian Ethnic Studies,* Vol. 26, no. 3, 1994, pp. 122-134.

NOTES

1 The study, conducted in August of 1995, was supported by a research grant from the federal department of Canadian Heritage. About 2,000 structured questionnaires were randomly distributed in the city of Vancouver, and 778 questionnaires from respondents were completed. Data was collected to see what economic and social effects Chinese immigration in recent years has brought to Vancouver, and how the public perceived of and reacted to the increased Chinese presence in Vancouver.

CANADA AND THE WORLD

THE ROLE OF ETHNIC MINORITIES IN BUILDING A STRONGER ECONOMY AND A MORE UNITED COUNTRY

Jonathan L. Calof

Canada has been referred to in international circles as a success in search of a problem. Why? Because despite predictions that we will lead the G7 countries in economic growth, and despite being ranked by the United Nations as one of the best countries to live in, Canada is in the midst of tearing itself apart economically and politically through the unity debate. At issue is whether Canada remains a single united country, a loose confederation of provincial/territorial entities or two separate countries.

Why should the country stay together? The economic fallout of separation, say many economists, would be devastating. But a strong, united Canada will, according to many, depend on strong economic growth, national, not regional pride, and a strong group of Canadians bent on unity. This paper posits that the diversity of our population, our wealth of immigrants and minorities, has an integral role to play in all these areas and may help to create a more united Canada.

A CULTURE OF UNITY AND NATIONAL PRIDE

In the now infamous post referendum speech, the former premier of Quebec, Jacques Parizeau, blamed the defeat on "money and the ethnic vote". National unity is saved by immigrants and minorities. While, undoubtedly, fear of their treatment in a separate Quebec contributed to their vote, pride in Canada itself seemed to be a major factor in the voting pattern of these groups. Talk to a recent immigrant and you will undoubtedly hear a tale of how wonderful it is to be Canadian. In roundtables on national unity sponsored by the Pearson-Shoyama Institute and the Canadian Ethnocultural Council, representatives of these groups have expressed a strong desire for a united Canada. What seems to be expressed by such individuals is that they do not take the Canadian quality of life (the best in the world according to the UN) for granted. Many have come from countries with low standards of living, political instability, economic hardship and/or lack of freedom. They revel in what Canada has to offer. It is members of these groups who have the hardest time understanding a debate which will unquestionably hurt Canada economically. Those who have come from Europe and believe that economic unity throughout Europe is needed for sustainable economic growth, cannot sanction their country of choice going the opposite way. It should therefore come as no surprise that minorities voted so overwhelmingly against separation in the recent Quebec referendum. It is probable that Canada will be able to count on immigrants and other minorities to put forward their best efforts to keep the country together.

Immigrants may have another positive impact on Canada. They are playing a role in the creation of national symbols of pride. The recent Olympics in Atlanta provides an example of this. It was with great pride that all Canadians celebrated the accomplishments of our team. In particular, our victory in the 4 x 100 metre relay race provided us with a national rallying point. These accomplishments symbolize national unity and national pride. According to some in the American press, they also symbolize Canadian immigration policy. In fact, several of our competitors and many of our medals came from minorities and recent immigrants. Much national pride is derived from the performance of new and recent Canadians and there are few areas in society where their impact has not been felt. Once again, diversity saves the day.

A STRONG AND GROWING ECONOMY

Immigrants and other minorities may make unique contributions to economic prosperity and job growth. Let's start with the opportunities created by an increasingly diverse Canada. The Canadian mosaic is changing. In the 1991 census, 42 per cent of all Canadians reported that they had at least one ancestor who was neither English or French, and by 2006, it is estimated that the visible minority population will rise to 5.6 million people. Further, the source of these "new Canadians" is changing, with the biggest growth being not from Western Europe and the United States but from Asia, Africa, and Latin America. Not only are their numbers rising; so too is their economic might. A recent Conference Board of Canada report noted that the visible minority market is worth $78 billion annually. This is solid economic might from a growing and increasingly prosperous group of new Canadians. These new Canadians are not only helping to spur the Canadian gross national product (GNP) through commercial spending; they may also be a group which is disproportionately creating export opportunities and its ensuing jobs.

Exporting currently accounts for 40 per cent of the Canadian GNP and over two million jobs—and even this is not enough. Federal and provincial governments have stated that a failure to increase our exports will result in a decline in our standard of living. The need to increase exports is so great that the Canadian government has set an ambitious goal of doubling the number of exporters by the year 2000. Not only is the government seeking to increase the number of firms that export, they are also focusing on diversifying the markets that Canada exports to. In 1994, 84 per cent of our export market was dominated by three countries: the United States, Japan and the United Kingdom. As was noted in a recent Conference Board of Canada report:

> *While these traditional export markets are, and will continue to be, profitable for Canadian business, long-term prospects for significant growth in these markets look disturbingly slim ... if Canada and Canadian business continue to rely heavily on these markets, our export growth and standard of living will be relegated to the slow lane of international commerce.*[1]

Thus, Canada needs more exporters and more firms who will export to the emerging economies. Both of these represent unique ethnocultural opportunities.

What are the export values of diversity? A *Business Week* feature on immigration and exporting summed it up well:

> *Immigrant entrepreneurs have also made big contributions to the US export boom. Businesses run by immigrants from Asia, for example, have ready-made connections overseas. Immigrants bring a global perspective and international contacts to insular American businesses.*[2]

DIFFERENT MARKETS

The emerging markets of the future will be in Asia and Latin America, the Pacific Rim (excluding Canada, the United States, Russia and Australia), representing a market of $5.5 trillion. China's capital market should reach $1.4 trillion within five years and Chinese imports have grown at 25 per cent per year over the past two years. India has been experiencing enormous growth in recent years. Between 1984 and 1990, the market for consumer goods has increased by 220 per cent. Why aren't Canadian businesses pursuing opportunities in these markets? According to recent research, because of differences in language, culture, and business practises, and because of an inability to understand the market itself. Yet for many individuals of Asian heritage (beyond first generation immigrants) the language, culture and intricacies of these markets are as well understood as that of the Canadian marketplace.

Researchers have long found that firms' first export markets tend to be those which are psychoculturally closest to them—that is, having similar cultural, legal, language and other characteristics.[3] Less experienced exporters tend to be uncomfortable dealing with markets not sharing these commonalities. It is for this reason that, for most Canadians, the first export market is the United States followed by the United Kingdom. No wonder, since this is where our immigration base has historically been from, and our population is largely English-speaking. But members from "diversity" see the world differently. When I was in the airport in London, England, I met a Canadian of Indian birth. He had been in Canada for over 20 years and his first export market was India. In fact, he had a production operation there. To him, India was not that foreign a market in the same way that, to many Canadians, the United States is not that foreign a market. The pattern is similar with Italy, the Ukraine and other countries: business people who have their origins in these countries are the most likely to engage in trade with those markets.

KNOWLEDGE ABOUT FOREIGN MARKETS

A critical factor in the ability to carry out international activities is having appropriate knowledge about foreign markets, techniques of foreign operation, ways of doing business, and so on. Immigrants and their offspring possess experiential knowledge about their country of origin. The need to adapt the product (though not always required) which has also been associated with better export performance, is better understood by a manager from the intended export market or one whose family has ties to that country.

Ask an experienced exporter what the most important factor is for making export sales and he or she will probably say contacts in the market. In a survey of Canadian exporters, the number one source for information was personal contacts, with person-to-person contact being the preferred means to gather information. Most international business textbooks stress the importance of the interpersonal dimension. As many experts have noted, success in most export markets depends on knowing the right people and having the right connections.

How does this relate to diversity? A *Business Week* article from 1993 makes the point that "with a global perspective and *ready made contacts overseas,* immigrants often start export oriented companies."[4] (Emphasis mine.) A series of round tables on Canadian trade with Asia came to similar conclusions regarding contacts in Asia available to Asian immigrants and their families.

Recent immigrants generally have contacts back in their country of origin. Their descendants may also retain contacts by virtue of family connections or community affiliations. These can benefit their own businesses, or their employers. For example, La Maison du Patriote, manufacturers of log homes, have sold six houses in Japan and have 30 Japanese customers waiting for more. The sales were made by a

Japanese immigrant who has a brother in the real estate business in Japan.[5]

How important are these immigrant-developed export advantages? Christopher Farrell's 1993 *Business Week* article was titled "Shut out Immigrants and Trade may Suffer".

SUMMARY AND CONCLUSIONS

Job creation through enhanced exports; creation of national symbols through individual excellence; and an observed commitment to unity through actions during the Quebec referendum—it is evident that minorities and immigrants may have an integral role to play in the maintenance of a strong federal Canada. How to tap these resources is something that we have to examine carefully.

NOTES

1 Taylor, Christine, "Dimensions of diversity in Canadian business". *Conference Board of Canada,* 1995, pp. 143-95.

2 Mandel, Michael J., Christopher Farrell, and Dori Jones. "The Immigrants: How They're Helping to Revitalise the U.S. Economy". *Business Week*, July 13, 1992, pp. 114-118.

3 Papadopoulos, Nicolas and Jean-Emile Denis. "Inventory, Taxonomy and Assessment of Methods for International Market Selection". *International Marketing Review*, autumn, 1988, pp. 38-51.

---

4 Farrell, Christopher. "Shut Out Immigrants and Trade May Suffer". *Business Week,* July 5, 1993, p. 82.

5 "Our Latest Japanese Export: Log Homes". *Canadian Business*, Vol. 65, February, 1992, p. 15.

MULTICULTURALISM IN AUSTRALIA, THE UNITED STATES AND THE UNITED KINGDOM: AN OVERVIEW

Karim H. Karim

The Australian immigration minister, Al Grassby, visited Canada in 1973 and discovered multiculturalism. He took the idea back to Australia, which also adopted the policy. Even though the manner in which the Canadian and Australian governments have implemented multiculturalism differ in some respects, both have continued to learn from each other's experiences. The last two decades have also seen attempts in the United States and the United Kingdom to adopt multicultural approaches. This essay looks briefly at multiculturalism in Australia, the United States and the United Kingdom, and discusses proposals for future directions.

AUSTRALIA

It is becoming increasingly clear that the international links of newcomers are vital advantages for immigrant-receiving countries in the era of globalization. Multiculturalism policies have generally tended to de-emphasize diasporic networks since their primary thrust has been to integrate newcomers into the national community. However, Australia's

Productive Diversity Strategy has sought to take advantage of its newcomers' diasporic connections to enhance its trade links. The Office of Multicultural Affairs has coordinated this and other multiculturalism programs in partnership with various parts of the Australian government.

Australia declared social justice to be a primary dimension of its multicultural policy. It also emphasized that the policy applied to all Australians. Canberra identified a national commitment and certain core values along with reciprocal respect across cultures as marking the limits to its multicultural policy. However, multiculturalism, integration and cultural diversity are viewed by some Australian scholars as pursuing assimilationist aims because they require adherence to the core values shaped only by dominant groups. Instead, they present "cultural difference" as a dynamic approach that focuses on the negotiation of boundaries between various communal identities; it is also seen as allowing *all* citizens to participate in shaping core values.

The Australian experience has also shown that partnerships can be forged between ethnocultural organizations and those that represent other social interests. Such alliances can better respond to the needs of the intersecting identities of individuals and enable simultaneous participation in various sectors of society. However, scholars have cautioned that inclusionary strategies also have to identify and deal with the barriers that exclude.

UNITED STATES

While the American government does not have a multiculturalism policy, a number of federal departments and agencies have developed programs to meet the needs of people of minority ethnic backgrounds. These include the National Endowment for the Arts, the National Parks Service, and the National Telecommunications and Information

Administration. The non-governmental National Multi Cultural Institute serves several federal agencies in developing their multicultural programming.

Governmental approaches to social justice in the United States have been manifested in the civil rights policy. Unlike the Canadian incorporation of the issue of racial discrimination within multi-culturalism policies, the civil rights approach largely views discrimination issues from a rights-related perspective. However, the emphasis on the individual that is the very foundation for civil rights has allowed for the erosion of support for policies such as affirmative action, which are seen as favouring individuals of particular ethnic backgrounds.

Although the dominant socio-cultural approach in the United States is that of the melting pot, the proportion of "unmeltable ethnics" has been growing. Despite the strong sense of national identity that many Americans seem to possess, most also identify with aspects of their ethnocultural and other backgrounds. The increasing cultural interaction and inter-marriage among minority groups has been creating a melange of cultures that does not adhere to the Anglo-conformity paradigm of the melting pot. Guillermo Gomez-Peña, a performance artist who lives in Mexico City and New York comments on the effect of transnational migrations:

> *The bankrupt notion of the melting pot has been replaced by a model that is more germane to the times, that of the menudo chowder. According to this model, most of the ingredients do melt, but some stubborn chunks are condemned merely to float. Vergigratia!*

UNITED KINGDOM

Like other countries which have absorbed significant numbers of immigrants, the United Kingdom has grappled with the issue of its national identity in the context of its evolving ethnic demography. Whereas the initial governmental response was to attempt to assimilate the newcomers, the current thinking leans towards a model that does not seek to impose the dominant culture onto ethnic minorities.

The management of diversity issues is decentralized within the British government. Whereas the substantial part of the activity is carried out under the aegis of the Home Office, significant work is also done by other departments such as the Scottish Office, Employment, and Environment. The Home Office actively works with local governments in this area. The Commission for Racial Equality is the primary government-funded, independent body involved in race relations. The Economic and Social Research Council, the arts councils, and the British Council also develop policies and programs on issues affecting ethnic minorities.

The British approach to fighting racial discrimination has been imbedded primarily in the Race Relations Act. This legislation has provided for anti-discrimination measures and the promotion of equal opportunities on racial grounds. The Committee for Racial Equality monitors racial discrimination in the labour market. A major criticism of the current legislation is that of individuation: it treats discrimination as if it comprised infrequent and isolated occurrences.

Since the 1980s, there has developed a vigorous debate between the British multiculturalists and antiracists. The multiculturalists see antiracism as being overly confrontational, and the antiracists criticize multiculturalism's focus on changing attitudes through education and information. Racism, the antiracists argue, must be challenged head on, requiring a dismantling of institutionalized *practices* of racism in education, employment, housing, immigration policy, etc.

TOWARDS POST-MULTICULTURALISM?

Traditional notions of national, communal and individual identity are currently being challenged in discussions on cultural pluralism. Globalization and the information society have added fresh nuances to this issue. The idea of "hybridity" appears to have gained credence in international academic and artistic circles. It refers to the intersection of ethnic, "racial", religious, and linguistic identities as well as ability, gender, sexuality, class, region, professional status, etc. These intersections are seen as forming fluid and borderless "communities" which make the administrative categorization of people within fixed and watertight compartments redundant.

In contrast to the 18th-century ideal of the monocultural nation or "people", contemporary scholars are confident that national solidarity will emerge from the plurality of discourses and identities. Such solidarity can be possible when national institutions are not controlled by dominant groups, and the identity of "the people" becomes inclusive of all. The emergence of this new national community is characterized by lateral relationships among individuals who do not see themselves as belonging just to one social group. These intra-national linkages are complemented by transnational ones that are engendered by globalization and communication technologies.

It is in the arts and cultural sectors that the notion of multilayered identities is beginning to manifest itself. Cosmopolitan London is now the site of experiments in painting, music, video, film and the plastic arts that are transforming the notion of being British. Minority groups in Canada and the United States are also using broadcast and multimedia technology to produce cultural materials for export to their diasporic communities abroad. Cultural agencies of the United States and British governments are responding by carrying out initiatives that seek to forge new relationships out of the plurality of their citizens.

Several models have been proposed by academics that would go beyond the current multicultural approach to foster more dynamic and equitable participation by all. They forsee the emergence of multilayered identities, evolving core cultures, intra-national and transnational linkages, use of the information highway to forge solidarities, and dynamic national communities within a globalized environment. The civic and democratic participation of marginalized individuals and groups would be enhanced in these scenarios which would provide the mechanisms to adjust to the changing social and technological environments of an increasingly borderless world.

Reactions to these tendencies have included the oppositional ideas of some groups that seek to limit the national identity to the "white" population (as in the United Kingdom) or to English-speakers (as in the United States), harking back to the older concept of the homogeneous nation. But the insular state that demands rigid adherence to its dominant characteristics most likely fails to inspire loyalty from its diverse population. On the other hand, those governments that provide optimal opportunities for national and global interaction probably enjoy the deepest commitment from their citizens.

THE QUEST FOR CANADIAN UNITY IN A CHANGING WORLD

Geoffrey Pearson

Canada is a rare example of people of different cultures and languages democratically united in a single country. That unity, fragile as it might seem, has made Canada one of the most fortunate countries in the world.

Some countries are fixated on power; they are, or aspire to be, great powers. Others specialize on some activity or product. A few search for political roles in world affairs. Sometimes the search is made to help unite a fractious people divided by race and culture. Canada appears to be one of these. Unity is a Canadian aspiration, searching for it is a Canadian speciality, and fear of losing it is a Canadian trauma. Chief Dan George said: "One of these days we will all be Canadians." One of these days!

We are not alone. Most countries include minorities, small or large, perhaps as many as 5,000 in all. Some states have collapsed amidst chaos and violence, as we well know, or cling to a precarious sovereignty undermined by a rebellious minority. Tribalism is now a favorite description of a global society torn by some 80 or more ethnic conflicts. Separatism is rarely a peaceful activity, although exceptions exist, such as Slovakia and the Czech Republic. But neither is separatism an inevitable outcome of minority grievances. People can be given a choice in democracies, and they can choose to stay together, although I can't think of many examples apart from Canada. We can be thankful for that.

Of course, we also face another challenge, whatever Quebec decides to do. The *Economist* magazine put the matter as follows four years ago, after the failure of the Meech Lake Accord:

> *Many Canadians will hang on to their traditions. But the two founding nations will count for less and less: Quebecers will diminish in number, and descendants of the British will be an ever-smaller share of the rest. Sooner or later, Canadians are going to become Americans. Too bad.*

Yes, too bad, but not if we choose to remain Canadians, a choice that will be easier, in my view, if Quebec is seen, both inside and outside Quebec, to be a distinctive part of a country made up of several regions, many cultures, three main peoples, and two official languages. One in six Canadians was born abroad, a claim that no other country can make, including the United States.

My views are influenced by my experience of working in other countries—France, Mexico, India and the Soviet Union—as a Foreign Service Officer. It was never difficult to tell the distinct identity of Canadian visitors, whether they spoke English or French or some other language. They shared the informality and friendliness of Americans without the implicit assumptions of "we know best" and "do it our way" of American culture. Some of us summarized our experience abroad in a submission to the Special Joint Committee of Parliament on a Renewed Canada in 1991 in these words:

> *Returning to Canada after three or four years spent in a great metropolis or distant outpost, as most of us have done several times in our lives, we have all been struck by our good fortune to be Canadians, by the incomparable quality of life back home, by the relative fairness and tolerance of our society, by the beauty and*

tranquillity of our surroundings. Our foreign missions are microcosms of Canada where we have worked together in both French and English and defended the interests of all Canadians. We learned how much we have in common and how well our particular skills and outlooks complemented each other. Some argue that our differences impel us towards the breakup of this country; we know, on the contrary, how much the blend of these differences has contributed to make Canada what it is and how unlikely it is that the remnants of a broken country would enjoy anything like the same future.

My view of Canadian unity is also shaped, as you would expect, by my father's [Lester B. Pearson, Prime Minister, 1963-68] life and work. He too served abroad as a young man, and later he was to play a significant part in Canada's rise to international influence and prestige. He believed that a strong Canadian role in international affairs had to be based on a self confident Canadian nationalism, and that such a role would in turn strengthen the common interests of all Canadians. This belief proved to be right in the forties and fifties; backed by a prime minister from Quebec, he helped to create a sense of pride in Canadian leadership around the world. One source of this pride was the wave of immigrants who came to Canada after the war—some two and a half million in 20 years. Another was economic prosperity; we could afford to play a larger part in world affairs. But prosperity had its price. It was one of the principal reasons for the emergence of the Quiet Revolution in Quebec, and when L.B. Pearson came to power in 1963 it was "national unity" that was his primary concern. It became, he said later, "the most important issue of my career."

He defined the issue as one above all of culture and language. He wanted French-speaking Canadians to believe that they were recognized "as an integral part of Canada", and he hoped to accomplish this by persuading them that French was "an equal language in Canada". He often referred to the concept of partnership between two founding peoples, or races, or nations, a practice that led to controversy, and which he tried to explain in his memoirs: "The French in Canada are a nation in a sense that they are a separate people." "But two *political* nations," he also wrote, "cannot exist within one country", and he rejected the notion of special status for Quebec. Instead, he began to talk of "co-operative federalism" and to encourage the devolution of power to those provinces which demanded it, especially Quebec. Such policies, as well as the creation of new symbols to express Canadian values—like the flag and the Order of Canada—managed to blunt the dynamism of the Quiet Revolution by meeting some of its objectives without breaking the ties of Confederation. But they could not achieve agreement on amending the constitution, then becoming an issue; nor did they overcome the basic dilemma facing the attempt to promote Canadian unity—the contradiction between the economic and social requirements for a central government empowered to equalize living standards for Canadians, and the political need to satisfy quite unequal provincial demands and responsibilities, especially those of Quebec.

That dilemma faces us now in its most acute form—the prospect of Quebec separation. It is difficult to believe that, in today's world, a country with all the advantages of Canada would have arrived at this point. It has not been for lack of trying to find solutions. Twice in the past eight years our political leaders have proposed arrangements that essentially satisfied Quebec's demands, as well as those of our aboriginal peoples, only to find that popular opposition to one or more elements of the package prevented agreement. No one now disputes that Quebec is a society "which includes a French-speaking majority, a unique culture and a civil law tradition", as it is put in the Consensus Report on the Constitution agreed at Charlottetown in August 1992.

But a majority of Canadians refused to accept the consequent changes in how we ought to govern ourselves, leading, as we might have expected, to the election in Quebec of a government determined to go it alone. Indeed, that government might maintain that its goal is justified by a second phrase enshrined in the Canada clause just cited: "The role of the legislature and government of Quebec to preserve and promote the distinct society of Quebec is affirmed." How is the distinct society to be best promoted? That is the question that remains to be answered, and whatever the answer is this year, I expect that it will continue to be raised in the years to come.

The people of Quebec remember, as they tell us on their licence plates, but what do they remember? I doubt that it is the motherland, despite the occasional efforts of some French leaders to remind them, nor is it the events of the 18th century. Perhaps it is the fact that they were "*les Canadiens*" long before the rest of us and that they are proud of the legacy and want it recognized. It was Daniel Johnson who confronted the rest of us with the slogan "equality or independence"—an idea that first René Lévesque and now Lucien Bouchard have re-named "sovereignty-association".

The current trend of federal politics, which is moving strongly towards more diversity and less unity, may in fact accomplish what Quebec wants without having to put these concepts into words in the Constitution. I remain optimistic that one of these days, all the persons in this country will stop worrying about whether you spell Canadian with an "a" or an "e".

This is a revised version of remarks made to the Annual General Meeting of the United Empire Loyalists in Toronto, June 2, 1995.

MULTICULTURALISM AS A BUILDING BLOCK

LINKING OUR MULTICULATURAL ASSET TO THE INFORMATION HIGHWAY

Jean Augustine

As we look at the Information Highway and the globalization of communications, we have to recognize that our multiculturalism policy and the "ethnocultural media" offer us unique tools to advance in this new age. We are not an isolated, inward looking country, wracked with xenophobia and afraid of the world. Our bilingual and multicultural policies reflect our proud heritage. The presence of the many languages within our population, combined with the human connections to virtually every country and culture of the world, have made us a cosmopolitan, outward looking country, always able to communicate with people anywhere in the world. The ethnocultural media has been our conduit to the world and now we need to take its legacy to the next stage.

Where existing ethnocultural media—newspapers, television and radio—allow us to communicate among ourselves and to the world, instruments of high technology such as the Internet can take us a step further. They offer us interactive communication, a vehicle for exchanging thoughts and sharing our voices with unprecedented immediacy.

The success of many publications among the ethnocultural media is evident from the fact that the readers of these newspapers are found in communities all over North America; Metro Toronto alone represents a large readership. The efforts to reach out and communicate in over 44 different languages to so many richly diverse communities within our larger national community are commendable. We should also recognize the unique and important role these newspapers play in heightening awareness among members of various Canadian multicultural communities of the challenges we all face as Canadians. Their cumulative efforts vibrantly demonstrate how Canada's third language media can address the information needs of ethnocultural minorities, especially those who are not proficient in either of Canada's official languages, and those who feel they are not adequately served by the mainstream media.

As Canadians, we are concerned that society affords each individual the opportunity to live and work in dignity, free from discrimination, intimidation or violence; that each individual is given an opportunity to participate meaningfully in the various aspects of Canadian life. Meaningful participation affirms full integration into the society in which we have been born or in which we have chosen to live. Integration is a two way street: It involves breaking down institutional barriers that exist within our society, and adapting cultural practices to, and values participation in, Canadian society.

BUILDING A COHERENT SOCIETY THROUGH MULTICULTURALISM

Canada's multiculturalism does not create division in society and promote separateness of individual ethnic identities as some would suggest. It works to build a coherent society with common values that respect and accommodate those diverse characteristics that have become a part of our collective Canadian identity.

Canada's multiculturalism policy and programs have been the subject of intense public debate. The ethnocultural media, whose work instinctively includes discussions of such issues, has played a strong role in directing this debate to a higher plane. Although Canada has undergone dramatic social, economic, cultural and political changes since the multiculturalism policy was adopted nearly twenty-five years ago, this does not mean that multiculturalism is obsolete. It means, however, that in order to respond effectively to our ever-changing society, the multiculturalism programs must continue to evolve. They must continue to address, in an efficient and effective manner, contemporary issues of full participation, justice, and social cohesion. And they must contribute to the development of a shared national identity.

The media plays an important role in influencing the way people think about issues that affect their lives. Ethnocultural publications play a particularly crucial role in providing information and analysis to their readership of approximately 400,000 Canadians. In addition, the ethnocultural media operate in radio and television. Our society needs clear and insightful conduits to provide balanced information to our cultural communities—in essence, connecting us and enriching our connection to the broader Canadian society. We must work together—the ethnic press, community leaders, and the individual citizen—to forge a shared and united vision of Canada and promote harmony among Canadians of different backgrounds.

It is also important that this branch of the media convey to their readership the values that underpin Canadian society—dignity, fairness, generosity and compassion. They can help us to better communicate the objectives of multiculturalism: to fashion a constructive response to the diversity in our country and inspire us to be the best we can as Canadians.

TRAVELLING THE INFORMATION HIGHWAY

As a nation, we have just begun to consider the impact of travelling the Information Highway and living in a world shaped by new information technologies. It is clear that competition is becoming more intense, that the workplace is changing. Many of us see that jobs are disappearing. At the same time, new kinds or work are emerging.

As parents, we worry that if our children do not embrace the new technologies, they will fail. And as they grow up in a global information society, how do we nurture their individual identities within a wider Canadian context?

These are understandable concerns. Yet, despite its risks and the uncertainty of its impacts, the Information Highway bespeaks opportunity. Properly harnessed, the new information technologies can be channelled in support of our individual and national goals of economic growth and respect for cultural diversity, social justice and the rule of law. Public sentiment, expressed in recent public opinion polls, suggests that we want to see ourselves and Canada reflected on the Highway. At the same time, we want to be "connected" to a global network and economy.

As an educator, I firmly believe the Highway is a portent of social transformation. As citizens of a common cause, we must ask ourselves: Are we going to be passive in the face of change or are we going to become agents of change ourselves? Many Canadians are already effectively routed on the information and related technology highway. As a matter of fact, technologies at which Canadians excel are already creating whole new industries. Jobs that we never imagined before are now commonplace.

Job creation in knowledge intensive industries has been double the national average over the last 10 years. Over the long term, businesses using new technologies will create new jobs faster than old jobs disappear. And that is why technology must remain close to the heart of Canada's overall strategy for jobs and growth. In fact, the federal government is responsible for 5.5 billion dollars annually in direct investment in science and technology. And the government is working to become a better partner to the other players in Canada's innovation system—businesses, academic institutions, and other governments.

THE 1996 FEDERAL BUDGET INITIATIVES

There were many initiatives outlined in the 1996 Budget specifically structured to enhance the ability of Canadians to foster growth and create jobs through technology.

These include:

- the expansion of SchoolNet and the Community Access Program;
- the launch of the Canadian Technology Network;
- and, most recently, the World Wide Web launch of *Strategis*—Industry Canada's largest Internet on-line business information source—specifically designed to help build a competitive and innovative economy for Canadians.

What is the vision behind these initiatives? What does it provide for the larger Canadian society? And what implications does if hold for multicultural communities? Jobs and growth, yes. But more, we want to build a nation where our children and grandchildren will be better off than their parents and grandparents. We want jobs and growth for future generations based upon technological innovation.

We can not afford to be left behind. We want Canada to be a nation where our children and grandchildren look forward to their future with a spirit of enterprise and adventure. And it is a nation where technology has become part of the solution to jobs and growth, not part of the problem. As a nation, we have complemented our natural resource wealth with high value-added, knowledge intensive outputs of the future. Canada, after all, is a nation that built a tolerant and prosperous society by turning our challenges into accomplishments. We are scattered across an enormous land mass. So this country became the best in the world at innovative communications technologies. Our domestic markets have been relatively small. So we have become global traders. This is a legacy that we—whether by birth or by immigration—have inherited. We must expand upon it. Together we must now work to leave to our children and grandchildren our own legacy, one that will incite within them the desire and enthusiasm to harness the technological challenges of our day.

We must work together to turn technological innovation and the Information Highway into jobs and growth for the future. And just as the ethnocultural media bring people from all parts of the world together by fostering communication, instruments of high technology bring people from all parts of the world together by allowing for interactive communication. The Information Highway will make it possible for people to learn at home or in a community centre or at work; at their own pace, at any time, at any age and any place in Canada. Here is an opportunity to craft a new mosaic to address the needs of the 21st Century, and it is within our means. In essence, it is our ability as an economy, as a society, to innovate that will prove our capacity to endure as a nation.

It is in a vision of ourselves as a people who find reward in excellence of achievement, who admire and esteem our fellow citizens who have climbed to new heights, who seek to magnify the qualities of determination, dedication, and applied intellect that we will rise above the dreariness of the debates that divide us.

This vision has been at the heart of our philosophy as a government. It is a key element of our jobs and growth agenda. And it is key to the sense of national purpose that we must strive for if we are to build a society of innovation. The choice is obvious—information technology must enable us, as individuals and as a society, to use technology for our individual and collective benefit. Our future is in our hands.

Just over a year ago, I toured this country from coast to coast as a member of the Human Resources Development Committee of the House of Commons, listening to what Canadians had to say about the financial and social security concerns facing this country.

I would like to share with you the experience, encapsulated in a very simple thought which speaks to many of the issues we face as a people.

> *The important question in life is not where you are coming from, but where you are headed. If you don't know where you're going, any road will get you there.*

It is clear that there is a road—an empowering conduit known as the Information Highway. Add to this our multicultural reality, the ethnocultural media and our multicultural resources and this is a highway we were made to travel.

REFERENCES

Paul Martin, Minister of Finance. *1996 Budget.* February, 1996, Government of Canada.

Connection, Community, Content: The Challenge of the Information Highway. Report of the Information Highway Advisory Committee, September, 1995. Website: http://info.ic.gc.ca/info-highway/ih.html

DEFENDING A MEAGRE PROGRAM

Amy Go

I tried writing this essay on multiculturalism in about ten different ways. Finally, I decided to write it in the most straightforward manner by first stating where I come from in terms of my analysis of equity issues in general. Using this framework, I will provide a critique of the official policy as well as my view on the backlash against multiculturalism.

My involvement in anti-racism and the women's movement has shaped the way I see the world and the way I think about Canada. In my view, poverty, injustice, violence and inequities are directly attributable to the imbalance of power in society based on race, gender, socio-economic status, and compounded by other forms of discrimination like disabilities, sexual orientation, religion, and/or culture. Canada has a long history of oppression perpetrated by white, wealthy, English-speaking men. Discrimination is pervasive and intrinsic in all systems and institutions.

I believe that any measure taken by individuals, groups, organizations, government or communities that is meant to redress the past and right the wrong should be based on a recognition of our inherently sexist, classist and discriminatory society. No measure will be effective if it is not based on such recognition. The official Multiculturalism Policy is one of these ineffective measures.

People have a different understanding of the official policy because there is a lack of will on the part of the government to promote it. Very few know that we have had the Multiculturalism Policy since 1971, which was upgraded to the Canadian Multiculturalism Act in 1988.

I am not going to dwell on the political background of the Act. I am more interested in whether it has achieved its purported goals and had an impact on society.

It is a piece of legislation without any enforcement mechanism, which broadly states that there should be no barriers for Canadians to opportunities such as employment. Although the Act "frowns upon" discrimination and barriers, it is totally silent on where they come from. The word "racism" is not even mentioned once in the Act.

Without incorporating an analysis of the imbalance of power amongst racial and cultural groups, the Act has failed the most important test as a remedial legislation. Some advocates have argued that ineffective equity legislation is better than nothing. Others hold the opposite view. In my view, the Act does nothing to advance substantive equality rights. It is, however, harmless in that it at least does not deny the existence of inequality.

Since there is no enforcement mechanism attached to the Canadian Multiculturalism Act, the government has the discretion to do whatever it wants to comply with the spirit of the law.

The Department of Multiculturalism was established shortly after the enactment of the Act, and was given the mandate to take the lead in implementing the multiculturalism policy within the government and in the communities. It was supposed to coordinate interdepartmental activities to facilitate community access to government programs and services across all departments and agencies. The Department was also responsible for public education to promote multiculturalism. It has been historically linked with citizenship. Therefore, it was responsible for promoting Canadian citizenship and facilitating community integration.

My criticism of the government's record is that it has failed to be an effective agent to bring about systemic changes within the government and in society. An effective institutional change agent should be well supported, not only in terms of unequivocal commitment from the top decision makers, but also concretely in resources and delegation of power. Without commitment, power, support and resources, the change agent will be marginalized as a window dressing measure. No real change will come about.

Unfortunately, the federal legislation and its implementation fits perfectly the description of a window dressing.

Multiculturalism has never been given the power nor the resources to enforce compliance. The only time that I have seen other departments show interest in the work of multiculturalism is when funding is made available to them as well.

The multiculturalism program also operates a small funding program that supports a wide variety of community groups and organizations to engage in activities that meet the objectives and goals set out in the multiculturalism policy and the funding priorities determined by the bureaucrats. Political interference has also played a role in the allocation of funding, most notably during the Mulroney administration.

A lot of immigrant settlement service agencies have relied on funding from the program for a wide range of community support services with a primary focus on community education and development. National organizations representing various cultural and racial minority communities also access the funding to facilitate community participation and integration. These programs are not the "song and dance" or "food festivals" that the Canadian public associate the program with. However, the impact of some of these more constructive activities is limited by the pitifully small pool of funding.

During the first federal Conservative term, the policy grew continuously until the 1988 election. Once returned to office in 1988, it dwindled in size, resources, power and status. At the political level, the Minister for Multiculturalism was demoted to a junior minister's position without portfolio when Kim Campbell took office. At the bureaucratic level, the department was dealt a deathly blow when it was lumped into Sport Canada and Parks Canada, in the massive Department of Canadian Heritage.

The present Liberal government has made no attempt nor shown any commitment to reverse the situation, but has continued the backward slide. The program continues to shrink in size and importance. In fact, it was made quite clear by Finance Minister Paul Martin in his 1995 and 1996 budgets that funding programs will be terminated in two years.

Although multiculturalism as a policy or a principle will never strike the same note for me as other equity measures such as anti-racism or employment equity, I am left with no choice but to defend it against people such as Neil Bissoondath, the Tories and the Reform Party because I am fundamentally opposed to their positions and what they stand for.

Their criticism of multiculturalism stems from, in some cases, internalized prejudices and in others, simply racism. They blame multiculturalism for promoting division and separation in our country. They argue that the policy achieves nothing more than the promotion of cultural heritage. In their view, multiculturalism and immigration policies are connected and equally problematic. First of all, the government brings in all the "undesirable" people of colour, then public dollars are spent for these people to continue to behave in their own ways. These policies encourage disrespect for "Canadian" culture and undermine "Canadian" identity.

Inherent in their argument is an assumption that we should all behave, act, talk and think in the same "Canadian" way, i.e. English-speaking with an anglo culture. Deviation from this norm, at best, can be tolerated at home, at worst, should be suppressed completely. The attack on multiculturalism is therefore very much part of the anti-immigrant and racist backlash that the right wing has launched.

Although I have expressed my disapproval about government actions on multiculturalism, I still believe strongly in state intervention in redressing systemic injustice. Government actions represent the acknowledgment of collective responsibilities of the whole society to bring about a true level playing field for all members. Without government intervention to mediate the power structure, those at the bottom will forever be oppressed.

State intervention, of course, is completely rejected by the right wing conservatives. Multiculturalism, even in its "mildest" form as stated in the Act still requires government actions. The Act states that barriers that prevent full participation of groups should be eliminated. This does not sit well with conservatives who are working hard to reduce the role of government so that businesses and corporations can prosper in a *laissez-faire* and deregulated environment.

Multiculturalism is an easy target for racist attack in the present climate of backlash and intolerance. In order to counter this backlash, anti-racism activists, including myself, have found ourselves defending a policy and program that we have trouble with in the first place. This is not unlike the social justice movement defending the social security system. The assault against the poor, people of colour, women, immigrants and other oppressed groups is so severe that our only defence is to protect the little that we have by at least maintaining the status quo. It has become acceptable to defend policies or systems that were previously seen as unfair and unjust. It is cruel irony to see that such regressive actions plague our country.

Why should Canadians have to settle for so little just to stave off having nothing at all? I do not have an answer to this or other questions. Let me conclude by saying that I remain convinced that concerted and persistent activism is the only way to help out of this mess.

REFERENCES

Canadian Multiculturalism Act, 1988.

Various documents from the National Action Committee on the Status of Women.

QUEBEC, CANADA AND MULTICULTURALISM: A VISION FOR THE 21st CENTURY

Fo Niemi

There is no doubt that multiculturalism is one of the key tenets of Canadian society and identity. With this in mind I will present my vision of multiculturalism for the year 2000, especially where Quebec and our linguistic duality are concerned

My vision is based on the realities of the present and the new realities of the upcoming century, not those of the seventies when the policy was first adopted, a period which the opponents of diversity so stubbornly cling to in order to denigrate or ridicule it.

Multiculturalism is not only about our present, but also about our future, the global economy of the 21st century. It is about our diversity—linguistic, cultural, geographic and economic—and our ability to be more than the sum of our parts. It is about harvesting our multiple strengths and developing to the fullest the potential of our social diversity. It is about sharing on the global stage our knowledge about respect for and acceptance of human differences.

In a global, knowledge-based economy where technologies can link people from one side of the globe to another at the touch of a simple button or a plastic card, multiculturalism is a valuable commodity or tool that enables us to culturally connect, linguistically communicate and economically converge.

Canadian multiculturalism means that we can choose to speak and understand at least one of our official languages—English or French—plus another, either that of our ancestors or a language that is fast becoming an essential communication tool in today's shrinking world, languages such as Spanish, Chinese, German, etc.

It also means that we understand and appreciate different cultures and remain eager to transform those cultural differences into new frontiers of learning so crucial to the knowledge-based economy.

CANADIAN VALUES

Multiculturalism expresses our sense of a collective history and heritage and a set of uniquely Canadian values that bind us beyond our respective differences. This is the most important asset of multiculturalism: it is a concept that is more fundamental to our national psyche and character than many of us want to acknowledge.

What are these unique Canadian values? To borrow the terms of Quebec's 1991 Policy on Integration and Immigration, which in my opinion was the most comprehensive policy adopted so far by any government in this country: respect for diversity and universal human rights, peaceful and democratic resolution of differences, solidarity and shared responsibilities.

Other basic principles have, since Confederation, helped bind this country, such as compromise and accommodation of differences. But, most importantly, to bridge this vast land and the diversity of its peoples there has been a consensus that strong and good government must always be present. The onus has rested on our successive federal governments to overcome cleavages, ensure minimal decent standards of living for all, and maintain a country that is more than the sum of its provinces, territories and communities.

It is precisely because of these values and notions that multiculturalism as state policy came into being. Government can and must provide a national framework to manage our cultural diversity, as much as we need a national framework to manage our linguistic duality, our health care and employment systems, our national defense, and our natural resources industries.

Multiculturalism is a Canadian invention and symbol much like the Canadian railways that link people and regions together. Born after Quebec's quiet revolution and Canada's centennial anniversary, its original objective and contents reflected the mood and needs of the times. Had it not been adopted 25 years ago, it would have been invented today, simply because the state of our country is such that we need a national social and economic contract for ongoing nation building.

In this context, multiculturalism is as indispensable as bilingualism: it is not only about the soul of our nation, it is also about the day-to-day management of our national affairs. That is, in essence, my vision of multiculturalism for the nineties and beyond.

There are thousands of people who do not share this view, as they fervently seek to reverse the course of evolution. They would harken us back to a time when this country was still a part of the British Empire, when the language of colonialism was the one and only great language, when the Christian God was the only God, when men wore no earrings and women wore no pants, and when people were left to fend for themselves.

Make no mistake. The forces of anti-multiculturalism and anti-diversity are real, they are strong, and they are well-organized. There are thousands of people in this country who consider multiculturalism evil: bad for old-fashioned values, for national unity, for individual rights, for balancing the nation's pocket books, for the French fact in North America, for the safety of our streets or even for the traditional nuclear family. These forces find their expression through a political movement, a national newsletter, a book and the information highway.

Many of these people are basically afraid of and/or concerned about change. They fear not only change brought on by immigration and the resulting diversity in their own neighborhoods, but also change caused by the aging of baby-boomers, by new family arrangements, by socio-political movements led by French Canadians, women, gays and aboriginal peoples, by uncontrollable economic forces, by the erosion of national symbols and institutions, by the fear of violent crime and most importantly, by the way our "traditional values" no longer seem to hold true.

Leaving aside the racism and religious intolerance within many groups opposed to multiculturalism, I believe that insecurity leads many to use multiculturalism as a scapegoat, because it has become so easy and fashionable to attack it. The saddest thing about this is that, by attacking multiculturalism as one key to the next century's doors, many people have neglected to address the real issues. Let me use some examples to illustrate what I mean.

We often hear people say that multiculturalism weakens Canadian identity and unity, since it encourages immigrants to keep their own cultures and languages and remain ghettoized among themselves. For them, one way to restore our national identity and unity is to do away with multiculturalism.

THE WEAKENING OF CANADIAN IDENTITY

This is a false debate. The weakening of Canadian identity and unity is caused by a multitude of factors:

- Budget cuts, debt and free trade have led to the permanent alteration of landmark cultural and economic institutions such as the CBC, Air Canada and the Canadian Railways.
- American products invade our television and movie screens, the Internet and our bookstores, leading to the irreversible Americanization of Canadian culture, albeit less so for French Canadian culture.
- The lack of strong, inspiring and courageous political leadership over the last two decades has allowed a sense of national cultural decay, not to mention ideological falsehood, to seep into our collective psyche and distort our sense of who we are and what we could be.
- Some of our political leaders have handled multiculturalism for almost two decades in such a way as to make it a divisive, cynical and superficial policy. It has been used for political appeasement and manipulation in many cases, such as funding of "ethnic exotica" activities in order to boost the so-called "ethnic vote" come election time.
- Since the adoption of multiculturalism in 1971, there has been only one French-speaking minister capable of communicating with and clarifying multiculturalism among seven million French-speaking Canadians who are generally mistrustful of this policy.

In summary, the weakening of Canadian identity and unity is caused not by multiculturalism, but by the lack of accompanying policies designed to develop and strengthen our sense of citizenship and identity. This lack has been compounded by the inability on the part of many to make multiculturalism better understood in both French-speaking and

English-speaking communities. Multiculturalism could have been better designed, better implemented and better promoted both at home and abroad as a truly unique tool for national enrichment.

RECOMMENDATIONS

There are things we can do to correct this.

First, we should explain multiculturalism according to the 1988 Canadian Multiculturalism Act, not the 1971 Multiculturalism Policy. The new focus is on equality, participation and inclusion, not heritage culture and language. The 1988 version of multiculturalism in daily practice even resembles Quebec's interculturalism policy.

Second, we should make multiculturalism a valuable export commodity. The expertise we have developed on race relations, diversity management and human rights can be exported to our partners within the Commonwealth, *la Francophonie*, the Conference on European Security and Cooperation or even the Organization of American States.

Our international standing on human rights, while not spotless, can serve as a powerful guarantee for our multiculturalism expertise as we export it to newly established democracies that must grapple with their internal pluralism. In marketing our multiculturalism policies and programs abroad, we can at the same time use the international stage to define and reinvent ourselves domestically.

Third, we must link multiculturalism with the new dynamics and requirements of a global economy. The ability to do business and socialize in different languages and cultures is a competitive edge for the marketplace of the year 2000, where value-added knowledge and networking will be crucial assets.

Fourth, we should dispel myths and decode code-words on multiculturalism that do not reflect Canadian history, values and traditions. For instance, Canada is not France, the United States, Great Britain or any other country in the Western Hemisphere, no matter how culturally mixed it is. Our country's history, which includes accommodation of the French language and culture and steps towards the recognition of aboriginal peoples' desire for self-government, serves as a unique backdrop to multiculturalism as we know it today. It cannot be automatically compared to other nations without putting in context.

Fifth, we must challenge those who call for the abolition of multiculturalism to produce alternative policies and programs on diversity, and to show how these alternatives meet with international conventions and covenants on minority and human rights. While a government has the legal power to repeal human rights, equity and other diversity measures, it is still morally and politically bound by international treaties which serve as the basis for many existing domestic policies such as multiculturalism.

Abolishing multiculturalism does not make the everyday needs and challenges related to diversity go away. Nor does it make us look good in the eyes of our international allies and partners who look up to us for leadership and expertise in diversity management.

DIVERSITY IN QUEBEC

Let me turn to the issues related to Quebec.

Quebec has officially opposed multiculturalism since the Victoria Conference in 1971. While many organizations participate in the federal multiculturalism program for funding, French Canadians in general show negative reaction towards this policy for reasons I mentioned earlier.

The situation is certainly not easy, since the issue comes down to protecting, for more than 300 years, the vitality of a culture and a language that are in a minority position on this continent. With a falling birthrate that already ranks the lowest among industrialized societies, Quebec also faces other demographic challenges such as the aging of population, regional migration towards Montreal, and linguistic tensions.

Because of these unique dynamics, Quebec society has approached issues of diversity and ethnocultural communities differently from other provinces. It is learning, after years of ignoring the issues of immigration and ethnocultural diversity, to make a transition to a pluralistic, multicultural and internationally-oriented society. That has not always been easy.

Former Quebec Premier Jacques Parizeau's remarks upon the outcome of the last referendum underlined the challenges of relations between the French Canadian majority and ethnocultural communities, not to mention those involving Anglo Canadians and aboriginal peoples on Quebec soil.

While those remarks were made in a most deplorable context—and were publicly and immediately condemned by most sectors of Quebec society—they did serve to highlight one evident truth: that the so-called "ethnic vote" is real. It did make a difference and it did show the increasing importance of a new demographic reality both in Quebec and in the rest of Canada. Ethnocultural diversification of Quebec and Canadian society is not only irreversible, but it also fundamentally changes the way we live.

Both federalists and sovereignists alike will agree that, regardless of the future of the Canadian federation, ethnocultural communities are here to stay. Although they will "integrate" into the mainstream once opportunities are made available, they will not forsake their other cultural identities, especially when the world is getting smaller and more accessible. And they will assert and demand their respective places in the sun. The age of "mosaic democracies" is here to stay. And so are international conventions and obligations on minority rights.

The choice, then, is simple: Should we leave it to time, chance and other forces of nature to manage our diversity, or must we adopt innovative, responsive and creative policies and programs that transform challenges into opportunities, tensions into harmony, barriers of exclusion into steps to upward mobility. The answer is clear.

I deeply believe that we can and must actively find compromise and accommodation to respond to the evolving needs and demands of the multicultural Canadian family. Be they the aspirations of Quebec, the expectations of aboriginal peoples or the evolution of ethnocultural communities, the spirit and values that guided the Fathers of Confederation in 1867 should enable us to end this century with hope, harmony, inclusion and equity. These are the same spirit and values that are embodied in our multiculturalism policy.

As we are about to celebrate the 25th anniversary of Canadian Multiculturalism Policy, we should not forget that our cultural, religious and linguistic diversity is an essential part of our common heritage, our common history, our common destiny. It changes as we as a country change. From time to time it needs a little lift and fix, but it is essentially like an old friend—with perfections and imperfections, yet indispensable, inseparable and unforgettable.

The ideals of multiculturalism will always be Canadian ideals. This country will definitely be richer and stronger if those ideals remain not only in our books, but in our daily lives. And that is one reason why a growing number of countries around the world have begun to discover and envy that great Canadian invention, multiculturalism.

HOW TO ADVANCE NATIONAL UNITY: A PROFESSIONAL AND PERSONAL PERSPECTIVE

C. Lloyd Stanford

I have had the opportunity to spend a good bit of my professional life in and around the national unity debate. I worked for The Royal Commission on Bilingualism and Biculturalism (B&B Commission for short), and after that the Office of the first Commissioner of Official Languages, Keith Spicer. I also worked on language policy among other social policy areas in the Federal-Provincial Relations Office, and helped to monitor parliamentary debate of the constitutional proposals at the time of the patriation of the constitution. I have also had a longtime academic interest in Canadian government, public policy and public administration.

When the idea of a referendum on Quebec's place in Canada became a reality in 1995, I was saddened and, as the date of the vote approached, alarmed at the prospect of a vote for separation 30 years after the Royal Commission on Bilingualism and Biculturalism had drawn the nation's attention, in its preliminary report, to the fact that there was a crisis in national unity. I was saddened because of the many brave steps forward which had taken place in the preceding decades. Among these, I include the political will displayed by Prime Minister Lester B. Pearson in responding to a pivotal editorial in *Le Devoir* by André Laurendeau by setting up the Commission under the co-chairmanship of André Laurendeau and Davidson Dunton, then President of Carleton University. One concrete result of the Commission's work was the enactment of the Official Languages Act of 1969. I would cite also the sustained efforts of Prime Minister Trudeau to reinforce the federation with institutional bilingualism, and "French power" in Ottawa, supported by the legal step taken to make New Brunswick officially bilingual. This process was echoed by parallel developments in provinces like Ontario. If the potential for repudiation of these measures through popular referendum saddened me, I was alarmed by the tenor of the national debate or the nature of the "political discourse".

The work of the B&B Commission, as it came to be dubbed, and the surrounding dialogue between proponents of co-operative federalism like the late Jean-Luc Pépin and advocates of either sovereignty association like René Lévesque or outright separatism like Pierre Bourgeault, helped to create an exciting, dynamic tension in the country's political life. Mr. Pearson seemed to move to renew the federation just prior to stepping down. His successor, Pierre Trudeau, started his tenure as prime minister in 1968 after a memorable stint as minister of justice. Interestingly, he was brought to Ottawa as part of a bargain with then commissioner of the B&B Commission, Jean Marchand, and was himself a former member of the Commission's consultative committee on research. This was a period of high expectations that the crisis in national unity would be resolved.

But it would seem to me that for all the insightful diagnosis of the B&B Commission and its concrete achievements, including the Official Languages Act and creation of the Office of the Commissioner of Official Languages to monitor its implementation, the proposed solutions missed the *nationalist* mark from the outset. This was my thought then and still is. For a fervent Quebec nationalist seeking independence, "French power" in Ottawa, theoretically equal status of the two official languages, and the strengthening of support for French Canadian communities outside Quebec were developments of no particular interest. In other words, these attempts to beef up the French Canadian presence in the federal political and bureaucratic elite, to increase delivery of services in French and the expansion of possibilities for francophones to work in French, were remedies for improving the federal apparatus. These had no political meaning for persons with grievances about Quebec's place in the federation and aspirations for its eventual separation from Canada. In essence, by the time the B&B Commission delivered its final report and the Official Languages Act was introduced (by John Turner in 1969), its recommendations were "*passées*" from the point of view of the deeper political crisis.

It is ironic, therefore, that so much of the national debate about this crisis, especially in Western Canada and in Ottawa civil service circles, has turned on the perceived bilingualism problem. The alleged predicament of "having French rammed down one's throat" has nothing to do with someone else's desire to be one of the "*maîtres chez nous*" in Quebec! It is simply irrelevant to the latter. The insignificance of this fixation on either individual bilingualism (which the Official Languages Act did not legislate) or even federal institutional bilingualism is highlighted by the fact that, in its action on the B&B Commission's recommendations, the Trudeau government rejected the notion of *biculturalism* and espoused a policy of *multiculturalism.* Several leading Quebec intellectuals of the day were disappointed by this attempt to separate *culture* from language: for them culture encompasses language and is part of Quebec's distinct nature.

To say that the attempt to strengthen the federal apparatus to serve both linguistic communities; to provide careers for francophones inside and outside Quebec; and to give practical support for francophone minorities did not answer the nationalist aspirations in Quebec is not to belittle the importance of those initiatives. Indeed, the federal programmes administered by the Secretary of State's department and the virtual transformation of the federal civil service from a "WASP" bastion into one in which increased francophone participation became the order of the day have had a remarkable and salutary effect on the country. In this, the Office of the Commissioner of Official Languages has played an important role of "watchdog" and catalyst. I had the great fortune to serve the first Official Languages commissioner, Keith Spicer, as linguistic auditor general. Mr. Spicer referred to the position as "director of special studies", to describe the function as investigations carried out on the Commission's initiative. I found it a stimulating sequel to my work with the B&B Commission in that it embraced everything from the ground work to monitoring of the implementation of resulting legislation!

There are several aspects of my personal life that also relate to this subject. I love Canada—I chose to live here although I love my homeland Jamaica dearly. I am married to a Franco-Ontarian with strong roots in Quebec (on the south shore of the St. Lawrence—Saint-Roch des Aulnais near Saint-Jean Port Joli). My elder son Daniel, lives in Montreal. He, his brother Marc-André and his sister Nathania, are all conscious of their French-Canadian and Jamaican heritage. We as a family have a great stake in the unity of the country. It's much more than a constitutional or political question for us.

One of the neglected aspects of the current discussion on national unity is the status of French Canadians "*hors Québec*". Since many of them, like my in-laws, have deep roots in Quebec, they probably have some emotional attachment to that territory. My impression is that, in general, their wish is for Quebec to remain in a united Canada, however renewed.

They certainly have been stout fighters for respect for the "French fact" in Canada and are sometimes impatient of comments that would suggest that they are unfortunately a lost cause of assimilated transplants. I would assume that a typical Franco-Ontarian, for example, does not feel like a second-class *Québécois* given the current opportunities to deal with all three levels of government in French, the provision of schooling in French and the improved prospects for the flourishing of the "living heritage" in literature and the arts.

But this francophone presence outside and inside Quebec is changing: it is no longer "*pure laine*", as reflected in my own family. This is a phenomenon with which both federal and provincial, notably Quebec, politicians should reckon. Canadian "governance" (to use the current buzz word) requires an understanding of social reality that surpasses an analysis based on the blood lines of the past. Francophones come from many different stocks. Today's Canada is a multi-ethnic mosaic within which multiple allegiances are fostered.

PERSPECTIVES

For me, and in various ways I hope for most Canadians, both the heart and the head are important in this great national cause. But the heart is more important. It's mostly an emotional thing.

An approach to national unity based primarily on economics is clearly foolhardy. Anyone who has lived the "nationalist" experience knows that it is not economic viability that fires the imagination of a group or collectivity seeking independence or a high degree of autonomy. The post-colonial or emerging nation model is the one to bear in mind when trying to understand and deal with advocates of separation.

As for the head, the main problem I see the federal government facing is the *political calculus* of balancing the fundamental requests of Quebec (based on the historical facts of the unification of Upper and Lower Canada) against the past and current claims of the First Nations and the other founders of the country. Among those were the pioneers of the West (including the large number of Black founding Royal Empire Loyalists) and those who have come to Canada in the late fifties and after. In other words, our leadership must balance *four* sets of considerations at the same time.

That is a tall order, and it would be presumptuous for a non-politician to offer advice to experts in statecraft (especially when the new Minister Responsible for Intergovernmental Affairs, Stéphane Dion, is a high-standing political scientist). However, I'll make a few gratuitous suggestions:

SUGGESTIONS

First, on the general atmosphere of the public and private negotiations, we should remember that Canada, as a multi-ethnic, multi-racial country, serves as role model for the world.

The world is in Canada. The changing composition of the population has triggered governmental responses like the implementation of a policy on multiculturalism (enunciated in 1971 by Prime Minister Trudeau as part of his response to the final report of the B&B Commission) which has been much admired around the world and imitated by countries such as Australia. There has been some controversy about administration of that policy and implementation of the resulting Canadian Multiculturalism Act of 1988. Attempts to move the thrust of governmental action from song and dance to a focus on full participation in Canadian society came in the wake of a parliamentary committee's report, *Equality Now! Report of the Special Committee on Visible Minorities in Canadian Society.* In spite of such controversy, the world still admires Canada for the relative harmony in which the various ethnicities live here.

Secondly, we preach and have traditionally practiced the Commonwealth value of consensus, based on compromise, in our foreign policy. So let's do so in our domestic life, especially now. Such an approach to the current crisis would enhance our already high standing in the Commonwealth in which, as elsewhere in the international arena, we enjoy the status of "honest broker" and for which we provide leadership by our functional approach to problems. It would also strengthen our credibility in *La Francophonie* in which we play a considerable role, based in part on Quebec's presence in our federation.

Thirdly, for both symbolic and practical reasons, it seems to me that, while the primacy and the immediacy of the threat of Quebec's separation is clear, it is incumbent on both Quebec and federal politicians to start using more inclusive language than that of two founding peoples. It is no longer merely a question of duality. The multicultural and First Nations issues should be part of the dialogue as one faces the reality of Canada in the 21st century. Indeed, serious preoccupation with the place of these other two groups in 21st century Canada would rebound to the benefit of both sets of politicians and the country.

At the more operational level, politicians must act in several ways, and some of the less obvious ones which they might consider are:

- Seeking advice from wise and experienced persons like former members of the B & B Commission: The Honourable Royce Frith, former senator and Canadian High Commissioner to the United Kingdom; Jean-Louis Gagnon, distinguished Quebec journalist and former head of Information Canada; Mrs. Gertude Laing; Dr. Michael Oliver, who was the Commission's director of research and president of Carleton University; and others who have thought long and hard about national unity questions.

- Seeking the advice of all members of the Privy Council of Canada not now serving in the respective Cabinets.

I hasten to add that I realise that Canadian politics have moved beyond what the political scientists call "élite accommodation", but drawing on the insights of those experienced Canadians, would, I think, be more valuable than consulting "spin doctors".

- Gathering and hearing from the best experts on the legal/constitutional, political and fiscal aspects of federalism. Canada has some of the *best* in the world. They could be called upon either to brainstorm practical suggestions on their own, or to serve as resource people to a constituent assembly. Persons like Professor Don Watts, former principal of Queen's University, and Professors Ken McRae, Richard Simeon, Peter Leslie and David Cameron come to mind. Regarding the general operation of a federation, Professor Cameron would be of particular value in transmitting the reflections of the Pépin-Robarts Commission whose model for the country seems relevant now. Among those whose experience in fiscal matters would be invaluable, I would mention Tommy Shoyama, former senior Saskatchewan civil servant and deputy minister of Finance in the federal government, and Bill Haney, also a former Saskatchewan civil servant and assistant secretary to the cabinet in the Federal-Provincial Relations Office in Ottawa.

I was also much impressed by the level of constructive commentary I heard on television in January, 1996, from persons like Mr. Justice Berger during the session organized by the Canadian Political Science Association at the University of Ottawa.

WHAT CAN WE DO?

On November 24, 1995, I heard the Right Honourable Joe Clark give the Ruth and Dick Bell Lecture at Carleton University, and was struck by several of the observations and suggestions for action on national unity he made in an inspiring talk and candid fielding of questions. One of the suggestions he had for us ordinary Canadians was that we reach out to Quebecers as individuals and express in our several direct ways the same kind of love and respect that was demonstrated during the previous October's mass demonstrations. This, he thinks, we can do through service clubs, professional associations, groups like co-ops or simply as, say, individual farmers. He also mentioned non-governmental organisations like the YM/YWCA, of which there are many in Canada. But he was particularly strong on the idea of youth exchanges.

I am not giving a partisan endorsement of the suggestions of an erstwhile opposition member, but endorse them I do and I think it is time for action.

SUGGESTED READING

A Preliminary Report of the Royal Commission on Bilingualism and Biculturalism. Ottawa: Queen's Printer, 1965.

Report of the Royal Commission on Bilingualism and Biculturalism, Book I: General Introduction: The Official Languages. Ottawa: Queen's Printer, 1967.

Report of the Royal Commission on Bilingualism and Biculturalism, Book III: The World of Work. Ottawa: Queen's Printer, 1967.

Report of the Royal Commission on Bilingualism and Biculturalism, Book IV: The Other Ethnic Groups. Ottawa: Queen's Printer, 1967.

House of Commons. *Multiculturalism: Building the Canadian Mosaic, Report of the Standing Committee on Multiculturalism.* Ottawa: Queen's Printer, 1987.

House of Commons. *Equality Now! Report of the Special Committee on Visible Minorities in Canadian Society.* Ottawa: Queen's Printer, 1984.

The Federal Multiculturalism Act, 1988

Divivedi, O.P., Ronald D'Costa, C. Lloyd Stanford and Elliot Tepper, eds. *Canada 2000: Race Relations and Public Policy.* Guelph: University of Guelph, 1989.

Spicer, Keith. "Manning the Linguistic Ramparts" in *The Ottawa Citizen*, Saturday, June 10, 1989.

MULTICULTURALISM AS A RESPONSE TO AN EVOLVING SOCIETY

Elliot L. Tepper

"Qu'est-ce qu'une nation?" Ernest Renan asked, in 1882. What is a nation?[1] His answer was short but evocative: "A nation is a living soul, a spiritual principle." The nation, he says in his celebrated essay, is "a daily plebiscite". What then is national unity? It is tempting to say that it is the eternal Canadian quest, always sought and never fully achieved, a work in progress for the country whose standard of living is ranked first in the world. However defined, it must have as its essence the opportunity for all in the nation to share in a common destiny. For individuals to cohere into a nation, they must have a chance to be part of the daily plebiscite, to participate in the common enterprise.

Canada, it has been said, is the first post-national state, the first 21st century state. There is much truth to this view. For most states will come to resemble what Canada already is, a pluralistic society, resting on diversity. As Renan emphasized when the state was still new, nations rest not on objective characteristics of religion, language or race, but on the will to exist. Canada has already recognized that reality and has moved to fashion a nation, and construct national unity, based on the building blocks of an increasingly diverse society.

What it takes to succeed in this form of nation building is the *willingness* to incorporate all members into the nation, and the *means* to ensure that it happens. Multiculturalism is both the symbolic indication of that willingness, and the practical means, the policy instrument, of moving toward that goal. Multiculturalism is all about social cohesion. It is about allowing the distinctive Canadian state to evolve. Multiculturalism in this sense is essential to national unity.

This essay will deal with multiculturalism as a social reality, as a government policy under duress, and as an essential element in national unity.

THE DIMENSIONS OF DIVERSITY

Multiculturalism is difficult to define because the term is used in different senses. It can be a descriptive shorthand for a societal or demographic phenomenon, a symbol of the Canadian state, the name of a government policy, and an agency of government. Debate is confusing as well, as people slip easily from one usage to another. Here we will use the lowercase term multiculturalism to signify the demographic aspect of the term, and uppercase Multiculturalism to signify government activities. Of course the two are intimately connected, as the societal phenomenon led to the government response. The two can be separated for discussion. But those who object to Multiculturalism policy sometimes seem to suggest that if only the policy would go away so too would the social phenomenon. On the contrary, the dimensions of diversity will only deepen in Canada. If the policy were to be abolished what would go away is the state's ability to effectively deal with reality. What would be lost is a primary instrument for defining the nation.

By now the general outlines of the country's diversity are well known. Perhaps it would be useful to review some of the highlights. As more data are available from the 1991 census, a clearer snapshot is available of the ethno-demographic bases of Canada society. Some issues relating to multiculturalism as policy and reality are also more clearly answerable. While politically, Canada seems to be moving away from support for diversity, empirically the country is becoming more diverse. Moreover, while Multiculturalism is accused of being a policy which encourages divisiveness, of encouraging lack of identification with Canada, the data show that the opposite is occurring. This perception, need and reality are growing farther apart. For a country historically considered pragmatic, not ideological, this is a dangerous trend.

There are several dimensions of diversity that are relevant to this discussion. The first is the sheer magnitude and direction of ethno-demographic change. Various indications are possible. A few are given here. Chart 1 shows the present Canadian "pie", and compares information from the 1986 and 1991 census. Even the few intervening years demonstrate the deepening changes in the country's make up. What is clear is that Canada has no "majority population". While figures may be added up differently for different purposes, no matter how you slice it, the Canadian pie shows "the other" as the biggest single slice, with a significant increase even from 1986. This year's (1996) interim census will show that the trend has continued. No pretense is made that "the other", the 42% of the population that is neither of English nor French descent nor a combination of the two, is homogeneous in any way. But the notion that Canada has a dominant population, with a few minorities to accommodate, is impossible to sustain.

Chart 2 shows where the country may be going in the near future. While trends often confound the academic fortune tellers, these figures are based on solidly established drifts in the demographic currents, and project only a few years into the future. As you can see, the large established groups continue to be numerically at the top, but their rate of increase is quite modest. Newer groups, on the other hand, show the fastest rate of increase, with the Chinese growth rate at the top with 126% and South Asians at 110%. Other studies show that while the

Chart 1

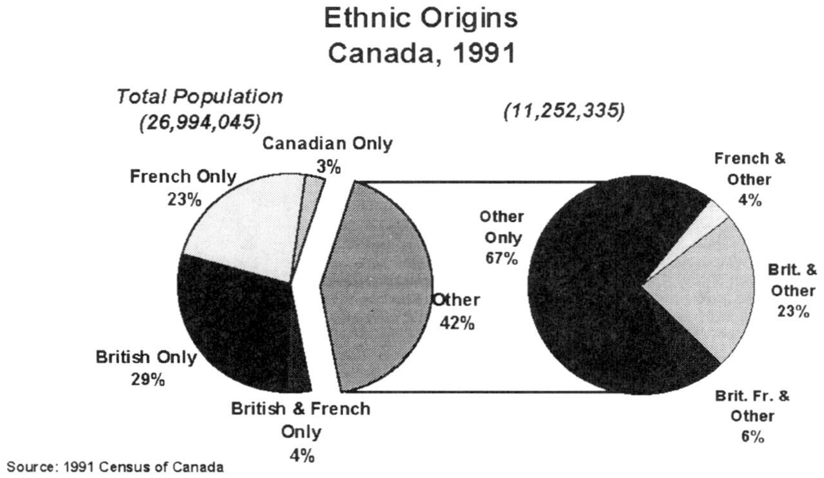
Ethnic Origins
Canada, 1991
Total Population
(26,994,045)
(11,252,335)
Canadian Only
3%
French Only
23%
British Only
29%
British & French
Only
4%
Other
42%
Other
Only
67%
French &
Other
4%
Brit. &
Other
23%
Brit. Fr. &
Other
6%
Source: 1991 Census of Canada

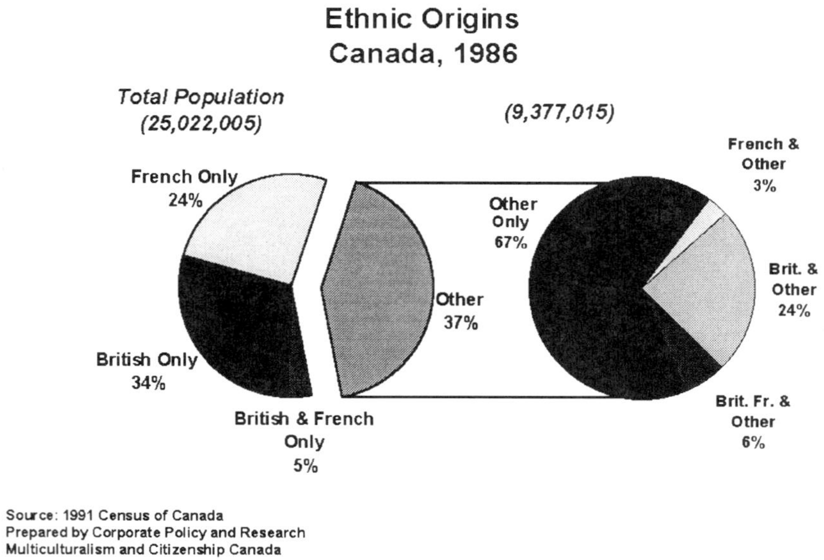
Ethnic Origins
Canada, 1986
Total Population
(25,022,005)
(9,377,015)
French Only
24%
British Only
34%
British & French
Only
5%
Other
37%
Other
Only
67%
French &
Other
3%
Brit. &
Other
24%
Brit. Fr. &
Other
6%
Source: 1991 Census of Canada
Prepared by Corporate Policy and Research
Multiculturalism and Citizenship Canada

total population in Canada increased by 9% between 1986 and 1991, the visible minority population in Canada increased by 58% during the same time period.[2] The same study estimates that with a medium growth scenario, visible minorities will increase from the 9. 1 % mark in 1991 to becoming 21.1% of the Canadian population by 2016.[3]

Chart 3 tells the story in a more compelling fashion. In a country with a declining birth rate, the country's children are a critical indicator of the ethno-demographic make up of the future. In terms of the number of children under the age of 15, the large established groups will either stagnate or decline, while the newer groups will show sharp increases. They are younger upon entering Canada than the existing population as a whole, and accordingly have a larger portion of their cohort in child bearing ages. Thus labour markets, consumer markets, school systems, and tax payers in Canada will be increasingly drawn from an increasingly diverse, and multiracial population. *Canada is a pluralistic society with ever deepening dimensions of ethno-demographic diversity.*

Another way to show how the country is evolving is to look at something other than race and ethnicity. Religion is something many people thought would be an obsolete topic in post industrial or advanced capitalist society. Yet as we approach the end of the millennium, religion is very much a topic of interest. The country remains and will remain overwhelmingly Catholic and Protestant, just as it will remain overwhelmingly white, and of original settler descent. Yet the dimensions of religious diversity are also changing. Here are some figures from Statistics Canada, based on the 1991 census. The religious preference of immigrants is significantly different from the existing Canadian population. In addition, the fastest growing religions in Canada are to be found among the non-traditional immigrant sources, and, as in the case of ethnicity, the children in the newer religious groups are younger than the children of those who practice the more traditional religions in the country. (See Chart 4.) *Canada will be more multicultural, multiracial, and multireligous as we enter the next millennium.*

Chart 2
Selected Ethnic Origins
Canada, 1991-2006

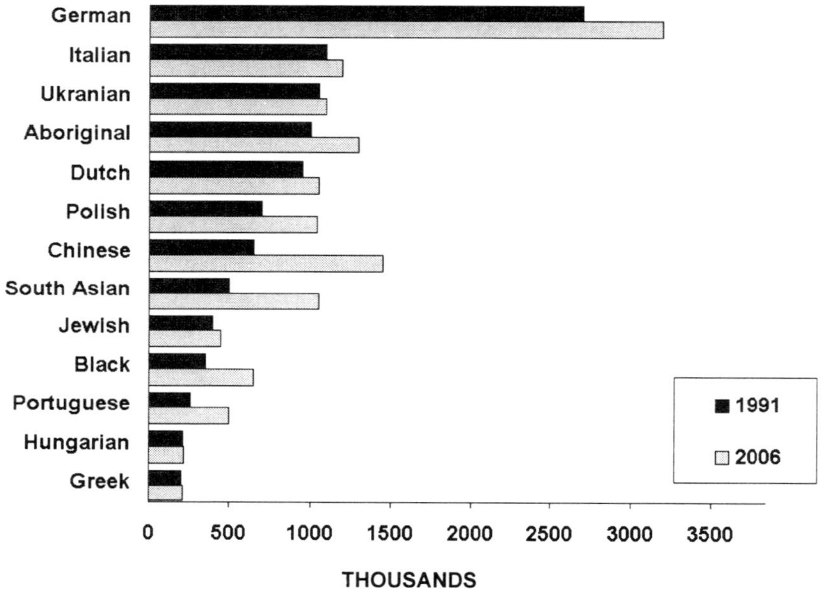

Percentage increases in numbers of persons reporting origins other than British/French/Canadian expected to range from 8% to 126%. Increase in large groups relatively small; German (14%), Italian (12%), Ukrainian (8%). Highest growth in Chinese (126%) and South Asian (110%), followed by Black (81%), Portuguese (67%) and Polish (44%) groups.

Source: Statistics Canada, *Catalogue 93-315* & *94-327*; Teega, *Population Projections of Ethnic Groups in Canada to the Year 2016*, Statistical Supplement; Secretary of State, *Projections of Canada's Aboriginal Population, 1986-2011*, Catalogue S2-232/2011.

Chart 3
Selected Ethnic Origins, Children <15
Canada, 1991-2006

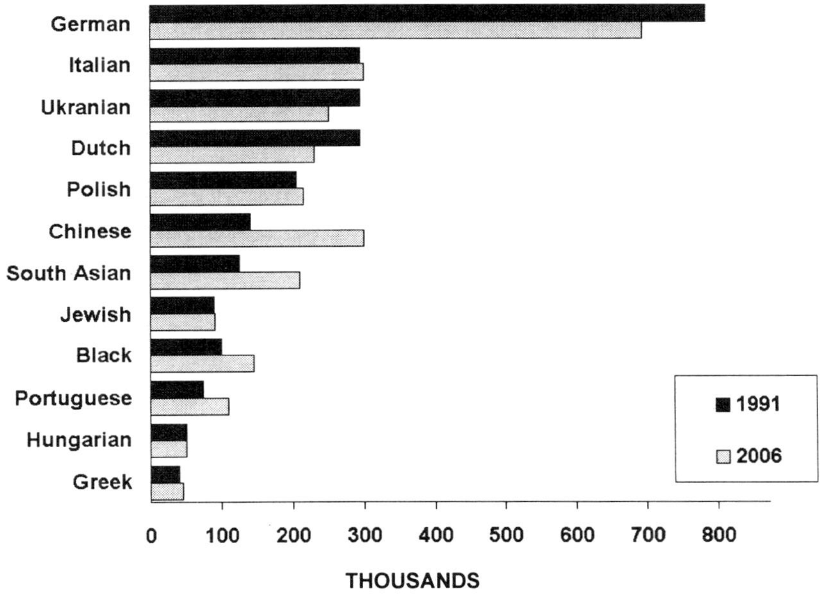

Percentage changes among school-aged children with selected ethnic origins other than British/French/Canadian expected to range from -16% to 98%. Newer groups show higher rates of increase: Chinese (98%), South Asian (73%), Black (51%) and Portuguese (47%). Decreases projected in Ukrainian (-16%), Dutch (-14%) and German (-11%) groups.

Source: Statistics Canada, *Catalogue 93-315* & *94-327*; Teega, *Population Projections of Ethnic Groups in Canada to the Year 2016,* Statistical Supplement.

Finally, what can the census snapshot tell us about immigrant adaptation? Large aggregates may be crude indicators of adaptation, but they are sometimes useful. Multiculturalism is often faulted for creating divisiveness, for keeping people in groups, and groups separate from each other. There is an urge to make newcomers conform to Canada, as if adaptation is a one way street in an unchanging culture, and to blame Multiculturalism for allowing minorities to not identify with Canada. The census suggests exactly the opposite. What common sense should tell us, and the census confirms, is that people come to Canada in order to become Canadians. Multiculturalism apparently allows individuals to identify more, rather than less, with their adopted home.

A high proportion of those who are eligible for citizenship have in fact become citizens in postwar times. Over the past twenty five years, since Multiculturalism policy came into effect, and immigration has been at high levels, increasingly from nontraditional sources, *the proportion of those becoming citizens has increased.* In the last census decade alone, the rate jumped from 75% to 81%. As Statistics Canada has noted, "most immigrants living in Canada are now Canadian citizens."[4] (See Chart 5) Indeed, while data is lacking on who the 19% are that do not take out citizenship one hypothesis is that many are from the United Kingdom and the United States—precisely those who do not have difficulty in appearing to adapt to Canada.

Multiculturalism as a state policy does not create diversity; it does provide a means to deal with it. With or without Multiculturalism as a policy, "Canada now has an impending rendez-vous with its polyethnic nature—the extraordinary ethnic variety of recent flows of immigration has altered, and will continue to alter, the old playing field on which the comfortable conceptions of the two 'founding groups' could play itself out, and indeed complacently overlook the real founding peoples conveniently sidelined on reserves."[5]

Chart 4
Religious Composition of the Immigrant and Canadian-born Populations

Immigrant

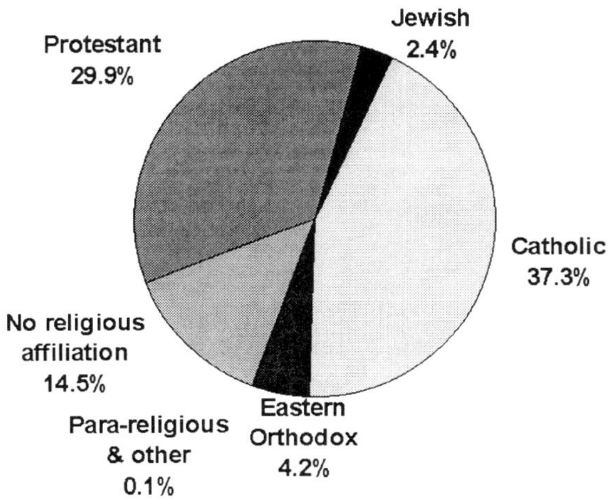

Canadian-Born

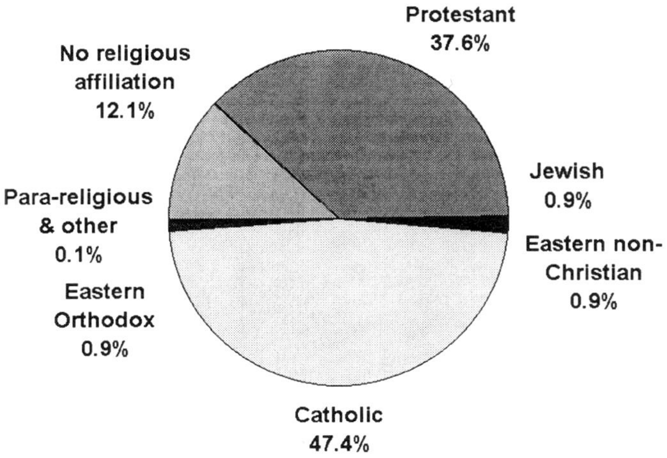

Table 5

Rate of Eligible Immigrants Becoming Citizens, 1981-1991

year	per cent
1981	75
1986	79
1991	81

Source: Census of Canada, The Daily, December 8, 1992.

GOVERNMENT POLICY

A short review of the policy environment over time will help place the present situation in context. Multiculturalism emerged in an era of accommodation and is questioned in an era of discontent. It was carried along by a wave of reform and is threatened by the undertow of retrenchment.

Origin and Evolution

Multiculturalism emerged as part of a larger process of change. The policy originated in response to major reformation in Canadian society and its self definition. World War II was the great watershed. It transformed the reality and sensibility of Canada. After the war, Canada reopened its immigration gates, which had been mostly closed, and racially based, for many years. Post war immigration transformed the country on the ground. Massive numbers of new migrants, the dispossessed of Europe, quietly altered the building blocks of nationhood in the 1940's and 1950's. Simultaneously, leadership of the country passed to the generation which fought in the war against fascism. It wanted an end to the divisions within Canada based on region, class and language.

Something went right in the postwar era. A positive cycle was put into motion. Returning soldiers brought a wider vision of the world, of the just and unjust, of fair play and the horrors of racism, of the need to sustain democracy as a bulwark against oppression. They also brought a thirst for education. Vast expansion of education levels sustained steadily rising incomes and progressive social policy. Public policy was about "caring and sharing", fair play, and ensuring that the forward momentum of the country was maintained. Canada went through an unprecedented and prolonged period of economic growth and social equalization.

Immigration rules changed to let in more people, on non-racial grounds. What could be called "cooperative capitalism" and "cooperative federalism" emerged. A plethora of social legislation provided for the long term social and economic well being of the citizenry. A partnership between civil society and its elected representatives rendered a transformed Canada in the post war era.

Some were left out of the progress. In the mid 1960's, John Porter released his monumental study of Canadian society, which showed that Canada was taking a different path to prosperity and political community from its American neighbour.[6] Canada, because of its different origins and political purposes was a "mosaic" of peoples, not a melting pot as in the United States. However, it was a *vertical* mosaic, a society of hierarchy and structural inequality. Ethnicity, rather than merit or effort, was the basis of societal sorting. His study made public the limitations of Canada's reordering of society, thereby confronting the country's sense of fair play. After the Porter analysis, ethnicity became an integral part of the search for an appropriate social order.

The Quebec question was unresolved. Historically, it was *the* central "ethnic" question in Canada, which was widely defined at the time as a compact between "two founding races". From the efforts to refashion the relationship among founding peoples came The Royal Commission on Bilingualism and Biculturalism. However, by the mid 1960's it was no longer possible to ignore "the contributions of the other communities", the theme of Book Four of the Royal Commission Report. Dualism and pluralism became fused together, as part of the new reality of a post war Canada.

By the early 1970's, the formula for a renewed Canada was in place. A far reaching exercise in nation building was underway. Canada would be a country with two official languages (to accommodate the historic dualism), but no official cultures (to accommodate the emerging demographic—and national—reality). Government would provide universal health care and an effective social security system, promote research and education, lightly guide the economy, and broadly set the tone for a humane and progressive social order. Culture was nurtured by the state, to flourish as an accurate reflection and supporter of the Canadian character. A new flag was part of a broader assertion of an inclusive, accommodating national identity. Later, a rewritten constitution would be put in place, with a Charter of Rights that symbolically and practically protects the vulnerable and promotes the participation of all citizens on an equal basis. Civil society, the real living and dynamic activities of a free people, would be given the safety nets—social and political—to construct a viable political community.

Multiculturalism can be seen as part of the Canadian approach to nation building.[7] As public policy, it is one way a government meets its obligations to its citizens. It was part of the process of reformulation, the redefinition of the nature and purpose of the distinctly Canadian state. The cornerstones of the policy are recognition of the reality of diversity, the need for equality, and the duty to protect the vulnerable. Riding the wave of change and modernization, the Multiculturalism policy (along with Bilingualism) provided recognition of diversity as a building block of nationhood. It is a policy response to the demand that fair play be a core value in a multi-ethnic state. Everyone should have a chance to participate in the experiment of nation building in post war Canada.

Multiculturalism in An Era of Discontent

That Multiculturalism as public policy is under duress is not news. What is less apparent are the reasons for the questioning of a policy which seemed so secure only a few years ago. However, there are a few obvious reasons for the apparent questioning of support.

As concern for national unity goes up and the economy goes down, toleration of difference wears thin. And there is a lot more difference. Immigration and settlement patterns are bringing dramatic shifts in the make-up of the largest urban centres. Women are playing dramatically different roles in the economy and society. Regions rise and fall in importance. The confluence of societal disturbances is unfortunate for policies of inclusion, policies which threaten older forms of status hierarchies and the self-identification of the nation.

The present economic downturn appears to be more than cyclical. It may herald a restructuring of the economy in unforeseeable ways. This is the only generation since the Second World War to feel that the children of today may not live better than the children of yesterday. The Free Trade Agreement and now NAFTA tie Canada to its neighbours in an unpredictable, and thus disconcerting fashion. The rise of Asia and globalization of the economy add to a sense of unease. Most of all there is the lingering high rate of unemployment, with no certainty that recovery will be normal. Downsizing may be a permanent condition.

The return of the Quebec issue, in stark terms, leads to concern that the country itself may not be here in another generation, at least in the present form. The whole prolonged effort to accommodate dualism seems to have led only to yet another crisis of identity. This does not bode well for those who remain committed to pluralism. Recognizing differences, especially the distinctiveness of society in Quebec, does not seem to remove the threat of Canada breaking down altogether. Removal of Quebec would mean removal of the primary hedge against a policy of assimilation, in the backlash against the breakup of the country. The threat to national unity is a powerful spur to the urge for an imposed conformity.

Multiculturalism remains the policy response to the search for equality in a plural society. Managing ethnicity, incorporating diversity into the equation of nation building, is the specialized responsibility of a small government agency which sustains the societal process of change, accommodation and inclusion. Multiculturalism is an integral part of the government's mandate to maintain "peace, order and good government". In an era of discontent, the responsibility is becoming increasingly difficult to sustain.

CONCLUSION: MULTICULTURALISM AND NATIONAL UNITY

Multiculturalism is a policy often portrayed as contrary to national unity. Government is accused of using tax dollars to fragment society by fostering divisiveness. Multiculturalism and national unity are portrayed as opposite ends of a spectrum. Critics of Multiculturalism depict it as fostering segregated identities, divisive, in a word "anti-Canadian". By fostering cultural retention, emphasizing what is different about people, Multiculturalism fragments society and prevents the emergence of a single Canadian identity.

Of course, just the opposite is the case. Multiculturalism is and always has been about fostering social cohesion. At the level of symbol and practice, Multiculturalism is about fostering an inclusive society, participation and a sense of belonging. As policy, it draws on core Canadian values of fair play and social justice. As practice, it has evolved steadily, finding ways to support civil society in the task of accommodating difference. It permits the creation of a nation.

From its inception, Multiculturalism policy has been seen as a government responsibility, directly linked to national unity. As government policy it was seen as a logical response, a Canadian response, to building a country on the basis of diversity. Here is how Prime Minister Trudeau first presented the rationale for Multiculturalism in his speech to Parliament in 1971:

> *National unity, if it is to mean anything in the deeply personal sense, must be founded on confidence in one's own identity; out of this can grow respect for others and a willingness to share ideas, attitudes and assumptions. A vigorous policy of multiculturalism will help create this initial confidence. It can form the basis of a society which is based on fair play for all.* (Statement to the House of Commons, October 8, 1971)

He returned to this theme when listing specific goals of the new policy:

> *... the government will promote creative encounters and interchange among all Canadian cultural groups* ***in the interest of national unity***. (Emphasis added.)

The themes of unity and identity are central to the vision of a multicultural Canada. In the response to the report of the Royal Commission on Bilingualism and Biculturalism in 1971, the government further noted:

> *Canadian identity will not be undermined by multiculturalism. Indeed we believe that cultural pluralism is the very essence of Canadian identity ... To say that we have two official languages is*

not to say we have two official cultures, and no particular culture is more "official" than another. Multiculturalism is for all Canadians.

Somehow the close connection between the definition of Canada and Multiculturalism has been blurred. A policy designed for all Canadians, to promote national unity, has been turned on its head.

The task of public policy is to keep some symmetry between social reality and the operations of the state. A gap seems to be growing between the increasingly multicultural reality of Canada and decreasing support for Multiculturalism policy. As others have noted, "a policy area that has had relatively meagre financial and support structures has been vilified as the root cause of such varied problems as Canadian unity and racism. The speed with which a consensus on the orthodoxy of multiculturalism within the political mainstream has been transformed into a rough-and-tumble free-for-all is breathtaking."[8]

If the gap is transferred from general discourse into the practices of the state, if policy moves away from reality, it would pose a threat to Canada's ability to manage its affairs. Too wide a gap leads to social pathologies, to high personal and political costs. Restoration of an assimilationist model, of forced conformity to a frozen image of a mythical past, is a recipe for failure in national unity. Only an integrationist model rooted in reality will allow the political community to cohere. Only a dynamic civic society, inclusive and true to core values of tolerance and fair play, will permit the political community to evolve.

To keep the country moving successfully into the next century Canada needs an effective policy for managing diversity. It needs a self definition of the country at the symbolic level, and the policy instruments, to keep everyone in the country available for that "daily plebiscite" which is the nation.

NOTES

[1] Renan, an important French historian, gave this widely quoted lecture at the Sorbonne, March 11, 1882. It considers at length the basis of a "nation", criticizing and clarifying common academic beliefs and definitions. It has come to be regarded as a decisive, if not definitive, exercise in definition.

A 1996 re-issue by Tapir Press of Toronto includes an English translation by Wanda Romer Taylor and an introduction by Professor Charles Taylor.

[2] Kalbach, Warren, Ravi Verma, M.V. George and S.Y. Dai. *Population Projections of Visible Minority Groups, Canada, Provinces and Regions, 1991-2016.* Statistics Canada, December 1993, p. 10.

[3] Ibid., page 26.

[4] "Total Immigrant Population" in *Profiles, Immigration Research Series*, Statistics Canada and Citizenship and Immigration Canada, nd (1996), p. 5.

The actual portion of residents who intend to become citizens is even higher than the 81% figure, as rate of citizenship increases with length of residence. The large numbers who arrived in the past decade or so will be added in even larger quantity to the citizenry in due course, but the figure cannot be estimated.

[5] Wilson, V. Seymour. "The Tapestry of Canadian Multiculturalism". Presidential Address, Canadian Political Science Association, June 1993, p. 7.

The complete address is available in the *Canadian Journal of Political Science / Revue canadienne de science politique*, XXVI:4 (December/decembre 1993).

6 Porter, John. *Vertical Mosaic*. Toronto: University of Toronto Press, 1965.

7 For an elaboration of this point, see Raymond Breton's "Multiculturalism and Canadian Nation-Building", in Cairns, Alan and Cynthia Williams, eds. *The Politics of Gender, Ethnicity and Language in Canada*. Toronto: The University of Toronto Press, 1985, pp. 27-66.

8 Abu-Laban, Yasmeen and Daiva Stasiulis. "Ethnic Pluralism Under Siege: Popular and Partisan Opposition to Multiculturalism" in *Canadian Public Policy*, XVIII no. 4 (December 1992), p. 381.

A MUST FOR B.C., A MUST FOR CANADA

Lilian To

The growth prospects of the 21st century call for global economic linkages and international cooperation. For British Columbians, this is particularly important because of our diverse population and our involvement in the Asia-Pacific region. Canada will regress and not progress in the 21st century unless we stop "multibashing" (i.e. bashing multiculturalism) and start enforcing the intrinsic values and policies embodied in Canadian Multiculturalism Act.

Let me explain my view by first addressing why multiculturalism is essential and then dealing with some of the myths.

MULTICULTURALISM IS A MUST, NOT AN OPTION

In spite of the backlash against multiculturalism and some political parties' opposition against multiculturalism, I do not see how multiculturalism can be abolished. There are two reasons why:

First, as established in the Canadian Multiculturalism Act of 1988, the policy embraces principles of equal status of all cultures, and equality of access by all. These are the principles and values entrenched in Sections 2, 15 and 27 of the Canadian Charter of Rights and Freedoms. The British Columbia government enacted the Multiculturalism Act in 1993 which enshrines the same Canadian principles and values. As well, federal, provincial and territorial human rights laws comprise the same values and prohibit discrimination on the basis of race and colour.

To "bash" multiculturalism is to deny equality of rights, to deny equal access and freedom based on cultural and ethnic grounds. "Bashing" multiculturalism will mean every individual will have to conform to one majority culture which is supposedly inherently superior; failing that, barriers and discriminations are to be expected. When citizens are classified as inferior based on cultural and ethnic background, when they are deprived of equal rights and access, resentment, internal unrest and strife often result. We do not want to see a repeat of the Bosnian tragedy in Canada.

A second reason why multiculturalism is a must is because cultural diversity is a reality in Canada. The underlying principles of multiculturalism are not only about tolerance, but about legitimacy. The policies of multiculturalism did not come about because of an influx of Asian or other immigrants, but arose from the Royal Commission on Bilingualism and Biculturalism. It led the government of Canada to recognize that a significant portion (now 40 per cent) of Canadians, who were neither British nor French in origin, should also be given legitimacy as full and equal participants in Canadian society. That was how multiculturalism came about. It is not about songs and dances. It is not about special interest groups. Clearly, today it is about reaffirming the legitimate rights of Canadians who make up 40 per cent of our population to be participants in the mainstream of Canadian life.

In my view, multiculturalism is a must because of the intrinsic Canadian values and legitimacy that it addresses.

SOME MYTHS AND FALACIES ABOUT MULTICULTURALISM

First, let me address the myth of hyphenated Canadians. Am I less Canadian when I claim to be a Chinese Canadian woman? I am proud to be a woman; I am also proud to be of Chinese origin. I can't change my background; I can't change my skin colour or my accent. But I can be Chinese, a woman and a legitimate Canadian citizen. I pay taxes, I vote, I volunteer at schools and the Red Cross. I even donate blood! Am I less Canadian because I am a woman or because I am of Chinese origin? Am I less Canadian because I also speak Cantonese and read *The Vancouver Sun*, *The Globe and Mail*, and the Chinese *Ming Pao* and *Sing Tao* papers daily? We cannot all be Anglo-Saxon white males. Multiculturalism recognizes the reality that there is diversity in society, that everyone is a hyphenated Canadian, whether they are female-Canadian, young-Canadian or Chinese-Canadian. Unless you produce clones or go through a purge, you cannot eliminate hyphenated Canadians. We all carry multiple roles and identities, and that can't make us less Canadian.

The second myth is that multiculturalism divides. The fact is that freedom to maintain and enhance one's own cultural heritage will not divide this country. The issue of "ethnic enclaves" is often misunderstood. The conspicuous congregation of Chinese immigrants in Vancouver-Richmond area in British Columbia has created racial tension. The presence of Chinese malls, Chinese radio and television programming, has created a perception of an isolated, insulated or closed community, and multiculturalism has been blamed for this phenomenon. But these are superficial fallacies. Please note these facts: Recent market research indicates that a large number of Chinese Canadians who shop in Chinese malls also shop in Safeways and Save-On-Foods. A recent study conducted by DJC Research indicated that while 64 per cent of Chinese Canadian adults watch Chinese language television, 61 per cent watch English language television, and while 74 per cent read Chinese papers, 40 per cent also read an English language paper. A recent poll indicated that over 70 per cent of the Chinese Canadians polled said that they would participate in the provincial election. I would suggest that 90 per cent of the life of an average Chinese immigrant in Richmond will be spent participating in mainstream Canadian society, working in Canadian firms. Their kids will go to Canadian public schools, their families will pay into the Canadian tax system, and receive services from the medical and social service system. Less than 10 per cent of their lives will be spent watching television, shopping or in entertaining themselves, activities more likely to be conducted in their mother tongue. How would this divide Chinese Canadians from other Canadians?

The so-called ethnic enclaves provide social support for new immigrants as they did for the Scottish, Irish, Italian and German immigrants when they first arrived. They are not building ghettos. They are not building a "nation" of their own. Multiculturalism does not epitomize a narrow sense of "nationalism". On the contrary, it legitimizes the right of every ethnic group to preserve its own culture within the Canadian context—this Canadian context cannot be stressed enough—and, at the same time, it ensures full and equal participation of all individuals in Canadian society, irrespective of their ethnic and cultural background.

I often like to use the analogy of a symphony orchestra. The violins, the cellos, the clarinets and others are allowed to perform at their best, to each maximize their musical beauty, but, at the same time, they all contribute to the success of the symphony. The "violin enclave" is not a ghetto and it does not erode the wholeness of the symphony. It is too simplistic to assume that the two are mutually exclusive.

Another analogy is with family units: these do not function as "enclaves" that divide neighbourhoods. We all live in some kind of family structure and in turn our families make up neighbourhoods, and in turn these neighbourhoods make up the country.

A third fallacy I wish to address is that multiculturalism provides special privileges to special interest groups. The key issue is that true equality and fairness cannot be achieved by uniform treatment. It would not be fair if the physically disabled were treated like the able-bodied and not provided with ramps and elevators. It would be unjust if young people were treated the same as senior citizens and deprived of employment opportunities or free education.

Under the multiculturalism rubric, employment equity measures are not special privileges but tools to remove barriers and ensure fair and equal access for all.

A fourth myth is that multiculturalism should accentuate similarities and minimize difference. The fact is that similarities should be recognized and celebrated, but the whole essence is to accept and respect difference. Only when cultural difference is accepted and recognized will there be harmony in society. I have a sad story to tell. There are reports that in some schools in the Vancouver and Richmond area, English as a Second Language (ESL) students have ganged up on both Chinese and Caucasian Canadian born students. The problem arose from the fact that some of these ESL students have been ridiculed and harrassed because they spoke English with an accent and dressed and looked different. Cultural diversity is a reality. Some differences cannot be changed. Unless these differences are accepted and respected as enshrined in the principles of multiculturalism, divisions and strife may become major social concerns.

To conclude, multiculturalism as legislation and policy is enshrined in the Canadian constitution and entrenched in Canadian values. Any miscommunication or problem arising from the implementation process does not mean it should be abolished. A revival of the spirit of multiculturalism is as crucial for building British Columbia as it is for building Canadian national unity in the 21st century.

REFERENCES

The Canadian Charter of Rights and Freedoms, 1981.

The Federal Multiculturalism Act, 1988.

A.C. Nielson Group (DJC Research). *Chinese Media Index.*. 1995.

"Our Dead Past, Our Living Present" in *The Vancouver Sun*, September 13, 1995.

Li, Peter. "Ethnic Enterprises in Transition: Chinese Business in Richmond, B.C." in *Canadian Ethnic Study 24*. 1992.

THE ONLY WAY TO GO: WHY MULTICULTURALISM CAN HELP UNITY

Joseph Wong

Canada is at a crossroad with its multicultural policies. One way leads to unity and inclusiveness; the other to constant bickering and friction, and possibly the break-up of this country.

Like a lot of people, I believe in fairness and justice for all. It is this sense of fairness and justice that makes me a firm believer in the principle of multiculturalism in Canada. As regionalism, and to a similar degree, nationalism, is on the rise at home in Canada and around the world, I have come to believe, more than ever, that multiculturalism is not only workable but probably the best way to build a country's future—especially a country as diverse as Canada—in peace and harmony. To me, multiculturalism simply means appreciation and respect for each other's roots and heritage. It conveys Canada's identity and characteristics. It implies tolerance, understanding, harmony, fairness, and full and equitable participation.

THE GLOBAL VILLAGE

Change is the only constant the world has experienced in the past ten years. Things that we thought would never have happened are occurring at a torrid and powerful pace. The political turmoil has given rise to a new political map in Europe and changed the power balance of the world. The world's economy has experienced similar shock. Huge, solid, blue chip companies are either sinking like the Titanic or scrambling to restructure to meet changes that top management fail to anticipate. According to a World Bank report, the centre of economic development of the world will be shifting to East Asia and Latin America for at least the next 10 years, with these regions' growth far outpacing the rest of the world. Within a decade, the World Bank report says, China's economy will be at least as big as the United States economy, and 20 per cent bigger than the combined German and Japanese economies.

CHANGING FACE OF CANADA

Changes in other parts of the world have brought changes to Canada. The immigration pattern over the past couple of decades has literally altered the face of the country. The changing demographics, though most obvious in big cities, are happening right across the country. The absolute number of immigrants, and the number from non-traditional sources, notably from non-white countries, have made much of Canada very different from what it was. The majority of the immigrants now come from Asia, the Caribbean and Latin America. The most profound changes are seen in the Greater Toronto area. In the last ten years, more than half a million new immigrants settled in Toronto, 70 per cent from non-European countries. Thirty years ago, only 3 per cent of Metro Toronto's population was composed of visible minorities. Today, one in four is non-white.

All indications show the present immigration trend will continue well into the 21st century because of our low birth rate and increased greying of the population. Increased immigration will be needed to maintain growth and a work force big enough to support the welfare and social service system for an aging population. Multicultural and racial diversity will be a fact of life in Canada for years to come.

THE PRESENT REALITY

One would assume multiculturalism to be the logical and natural outcome in the evolution of the country, given Canada's history, the many First Nations and the generations of immigrants from different parts of the world. However, I have been alarmed by the rising intolerance and xenophobia, and sometimes outright hostilities and racist incidents against immigrants and minorities across the country in the last few years of lingering economic slow down and persistently high unemployment. It has never failed in Canadian history that, in tough economic times, Canadians find scapegoats in the newer immigrant communities. We are a nation of immigrants who hate immigrants. With the new economic reality and political wind sweeping across the country, the spirit of generosity is being replaced by a spirit of narrowness and meanness. Study after study has shown that, as a group, immigrants create at least as many jobs as they take, and contribute more in taxes than they receive in services and benefits. Federal statistics confirm that refugees and immigrants commit proportionately fewer crimes than local-born Canadians. Despite all these facts, a myth is being perpetuated: refugees are associated with crime, and immigrants are linked with every ill of this country, from high unemployment to high deficit. The worst is that some politicians are making political hay out of this ugly situation by fanning the flame of intolerance and legitimizing these sentiments. For the first time in recent history, a political party actually campaigned in the October 1993 federal election on an anti-immigration platform, advocating a sharp reduction in the number of immigrants, especially from non-European countries. Very often, one will find racism as the true underlying motive behind the arguments against immigration and multiculturalism.

In the new economic and political reality of the 1990s, a lot of people are facing very tough times. Sometimes it's easy and even tempting to forget and abandon the poor, the old, the abused, and the less fortunate. Other times it's easy to accept and hide behind the excuse of deficit reduction and budget cuts to dismantle programs which help the disadvantaged minorities in our community. We should not pass on to future generations a mean-spirited society. We have to continue to speak out for those who are not able to make themselves heard, and to defend those who are least able to protect themselves. A society is only great because its citizens are willing to share their blessings.

PURSUING THE MULTICULTURAL REALITY

This is a challenging time. More than ever, we need to set our sights straight and affirm our resolve to put our vision on the broader horizon, and a longer term view of our future. More than ever, we need multiculturalism which is both idealistic and practical, and without which we cannot hope to achieve unity and long-term stability which is vital to a prosperous economy.

Multiculturalism has failed in the last two and a half decades in Canada because it has been marginalized by politicians and the mainstream business sector. Politicians have been using the policies of multiculturalism to patronize minority communities for their own gain, paying only lip service to the real needs of the people. In order for multiculturalism to succeed, all major stakeholder groups, including the communities, the business sector, and the governments, have to accept it and put it into practice.

It is important for the business sector to realize that multiculturalism reflects the reality of Canada, but also has a lot to do with their bottom line. A true believer and practitioner of multiculturalism benefits in several ways: employees are hired from the talented in the wider community, rather than from just a minor sector; the diversity of employees can better serve the diverse customer base and thus increase business opportunities; it creates an environment for harmony in the workplace, directing positive energy into growth and increased productivity.

I believe multiculturalism is the best way to achieve Canadian unity. It is time to re-establish a broad vision for our country. Blaming the weak, punishing the poor, or driving wedges among people is no solution.

Canada, as a nation, has been built by waves of immigrants at different time periods. Each wave of immigration, like a puzzle piece, is an essential part of what makes Canada a whole country. Our nation owes much of its greatness to the diversity of peoples and cultures from different parts of the world. The diversity of cultures enriches Canada. It also helps Canada to better understand and build bridges to our trading partners around the globe. Many people talk about the "Pacific Century". To its credit, the federal government is designating 1997 as Canada's Year of the Asia-Pacific. I believe Canada's Year of the Caribbean and Latin America will not be far behind!

While it appears that we have all the necessary ingredients of success, we seem to be unable to make things happen. Our immigration system allows us to choose the cream of the crop from other nations. But where are they after they arrive in Canada? Look at our corporate boardrooms, at the people around the decision-making tables, and upper management. Have we bypassed some of these people for promotion because of systemic and institutional racism? These peoples' expertise, talents, knowledge, and connectedness have never been fully utilized. Many were successful in their country of origin, and may have useful perspectives that are very different from Canadians. Have their views been sought in the discussions and in the decision-making process in order to achieve a breakthrough? The status quo does not work anymore in a rapidly changing world. It is time for bold steps.

Some people argue that with multiculturalism, Canada cannot develop an identity. I hold the opposite view. To deny Canada's bilingual and multicultural reality is to deny Canadians their fundamental national identity. Only with multiculturalism can Canada boast a unique character and a distinct society, like no other in the world.

CONCLUSION

Despite all the apparent differences in cultural background, heritage and skin colour, we have far more in common: pursuit of freedom, democracy, and human rights, and the love of Canada. While we appreciate our differences, we also celebrate our common bonds and our commitments to each other as human beings. Although the voyage towards true multiculturalism is difficult, it is also tremendously rewarding.

CONTRIBUTORS

IRVING ABELLA is a professor of history at York University and has authored many books, including *Coat of Many Colours: Two Centuries of Jewish Life in Canada.* He was president of the Canadian Jewish Congress from 1992 to 1995 and is chair of the Holocaust Documentation Project.

AMELITA ARMIT, a senior public servant, is executive director of Corporate Management and secretary general to the federal Public Service Commission. Prior to that she was an assistant deputy minister in various departments with the governments of Canada and Alberta.

JEAN AUGUSTINE was elected as the Liberal Member of Parliament for the Toronto area riding of Etobicoke-Lakeshore in 1993. She has been a primary school principal and president of the Metropolitan Toronto Housing Authority. She has been active in the Urban Alliance on Race Relations and the Congress of Black Women.

EMILIO BINAVINCE, a constitutional lawyer, is president of the Minority Advocacy and Research Council. He received his LL.M. at Harvard University Law School and has taught law at the University of

Ottawa. He is also general counsel to the Canadian Ethnocultural Council.

CLIFF BREITKREUZ was elected as the Member of Parliament for the Alberta riding of Yellowhead in 1993 and is the Reform Party critic for Agriculture. Prior to being elected, he worked as a teacher and a farmer.

JAN BROWN was elected as a Reform Party candidate for the riding of Calgary Southeast in 1993, but left the party in 1996 to sit as an independent. She has since become a member of the Progressive Conservative Party of Canada. Prior to entering politics she was an educator and business person.

JONATHAN CALOF is a professor of international business at the Faculty of Administration at the University of Ottawa. He is a member of the Academic Advisory Board of the Pearson-Shoyama Institute and is chair of the Community Relations Committee of the Ottawa Jewish Community Council.

ANDREW CARDOZO is president of the Pearson-Shoyama Institute, a regular columnist with the *Toronto Star* and an editorial board member of *Canadian Forum* magazine. He is a past executive director of the Canadian Ethnocultural Council.

SIMON DE JONG is the New Democratic Party Member of Parliament for Regina Qu'appelle and first elected in 1979. He serves as party critic for Canadian Heritage, Citizenship and Immigration.

HEDY FRY is the Secretary of State for Multiculturalism and the Status of Women, and was elected as Member of Parliament for Vancouver Centre in 1993. She is a physician and a past president of the B.C. Medical Association.

CHRISTIAN GAGNON is the Member of Parliament for the riding of Quebec and is the Bloc Québécois critic for the Status of Women and Multiculturalism. Prior to her election in 1993 she was a real estate agent.

AMY GO is a prominent anti-racist activist and feminist. She is chair of the board of directors of the Chinese Canadian National Council, a member of the Public Policy Advisory Board of the Pearson-Shoyama Institute, and serves on the national executive of the National Action Committee on the Status of Women.

NATHAN GREENFIELD teaches English at Ottawa's Algonquin College and is a pop culture historian for the CBC program *Definitely Not the Opera.* He writes book reviews for various publications, including the *Ottawa Citizen*, and is books editor for *Ottawa X-Press.*

KARIM H. KARIM is a senior researcher at the International Comparative Research Group, Department of Canadian Heritage. He has published extensively on minority portrayals in the media and the cultural history of Muslim societies.

NOËL KINSELLA is the Progressive Senator for Fredericton-York Sunbury, New Brunswick. He was the first deputy minister of the former Department of Multuralism and Citizenship, prior to which he was chair of the New Brunswick Human Rights Commission.

GABRIELLE NISHIGUCHI is a board member of the Ottawa Japanese Community Association and chairs the group's Historical Preservation Committee. She is currently writing a book about the 1946 deportations of Canadians of Japanese ancestry.

LOUIS MUSTO is a marketing and communications analyst and a former research officer for the Canadian Ethnocultural Council. He is an executive member of the Pearson-Shoyama Institute.

FO NIEMI is executive director of the Centre for Research-Action on Race Relations in Montreal, a board member of the Court Challenges Program and a member of the Public Policy Advisory Board of the Pearson-Shoyama Institute.

GEOFFREY PEARSON is a retired diplomat and former Canadian ambassador to the Soviet Union. He was executive director of the Canadian Institute for International Peace and Security from 1984 to 1988.

LLOYD STANFORD is president of the consulting firm Le Group Stanford. He sits on the Board of Governors of Carleton University and is a member of the Public Policy Advisory Board of the Pearson-Shoyama Institute.

ELLIOTT TEPPER is a professor of political science at Carleton University. His areas of specialty include human rights, race relations and multiculturalism as well as international development and regional cooperation.

LILIAN TO is executive director of the SUCCESS (United Chinese Cultural and Education Service Society), a major Chinese Canadian immigrant service agency in Vancouver. She is an executive member of the Pearson-Shoyama Institute and a board member of the Canadian Red Cross.

JOSEPH WONG is co-chair of the Harmony Movement. A medical doctor, he is past chair of the United Way of Metro Toronto and founding president of the Chinese Canadian National Council.

LI ZONG is an assistant professor of sociology at the University of Saskatchewan in Saskatoon. His areas of research include social stratification and race and ethnic relations. He is author of several articles dealing with race and racism.